How to Achieve Total Enlightenment

How to Achieve Total Enlightenment

A Practical Guide to the Meaning of Life

SAM MARTIN

Andrews McMeel
Publishing

Kansas City

05 06 07 08 09   RR2   10 9 8 7 6 5 4 3 2 1

Library of Congress Cataloging-in-Publication Data
Martin, Samuel D.
How to achieve total enlightenment : a practical guide to the meaning of life /
    Sam Martin.
        p. cm.
    ISBN 0-7407-5034-8
    1. Religious life. 2. Meaning (Philosophy)—Religious aspects. I. Title.
    BL624.M3484 2005
    204'.4—dc22

                                                    2004066003

Design and composition by Kelly & Company, Lee's Summit, Missouri

This book is for the entertainment and edification of its readers. While reasonable care has been exercised with respect to its accuracy, the publisher and the author assume no responsibility for errors or omissions in its content. Nor do we assume liability for any damages resulting from the use of the information presented here. The publisher and the author disclaim any liability for injury that may result from the use, proper or improper, of the information contained in this book. We do not guarantee that the information contained herein is complete, safe, or accurate, nor should it be considered a substitute for your good judgment and common sense.

ATTENTION: SCHOOLS AND BUSINESSES

Andrews McMeel books are available at quantity discounts with bulk purchase for educational, business, or sales promotional use. For information, please write to: Special Sales Department, Andrews McMeel Publishing, 4520 Main Street, Kansas City, Missouri 64111.

For Denise

Contents

[M]y own idea of freedom [is] the possibility and prospect of "free life," traveling light, without clinging or despising, in calm acceptance of everything that comes; free because without defenses, free not in an adolescent way, with no restraints, but in the sense of the Tibetan Buddhist's "crazy wisdom," of Camus's "leap into the absurd" that occurs within a life of limitations. The absurdity of a life that may well end before one understands it does not relieve one of the duty . . . to live it through as bravely and as generously as possible.

—PETER MATTHIESSEN, *The Snow Leopard*

And I said, "Hey, Lama, hey, how about a little something, you know, for the effort, you know?" And he says, "Oh, there won't be any money, but when you die, on your deathbed, you will receive total consciousness." So I got that goin' for me. Which is nice.

—BILL MURRAY, *Caddyshack*

Life can only be understood backwards, but it must be lived forwards.

—SØREN KIERKEGAARD

Introduction

As a young man I did a lot of searching, for it seems I was lost at a very young age. Of course, my early feelings of disassociation from the world can be attributed to all the usual suspects—a zillion different schools and hometowns, the absence of a father figure, an obsession with Space Invaders—but I think it had more to do with the fact that early on I knew that in order for me to become whatever it was I was going to be, I first had to discover who I was.

For many years, I dutifully searched in beer cans, whiskey bottles, and a grab bag of other mind-numbing diversions. It was fun, no doubt about it, but the fun receded when, after several years, I still hadn't found anything of note save for a few incriminating journal pages, some bad hangovers, and one pretty cool after-hours club in Williamsburg, Brooklyn.

So I turned to literature. In books by authors from Shakespeare to Allen Ginsberg I discovered what it meant to live an inspired, soulful life full of experience and gusto.

Of course, reading about someone else's meaningful moments and experiencing them for yourself are two very different things. That's why I knew I had to put the books down and, like Jack Kerouac, hit the road. My first stop was Nantucket Island, Massachusetts, where I worked as a housepainter and a waiter and saved enough money to backpack through seven countries in Europe. A couple of years later I visited nearly the whole of Central America and a year after that I bounded off for Australia, Thailand, Indonesia, the Philippines, Nepal, and Canada. At first, I traveled to see museums and the graves of my literary heroes. Then I traveled to get to know foreign cultures. In the end, I traveled just to see how far away I could get. As Kahlil Gibran, the Persian poet, wrote, I was "throwing myself into the lap of the Gods just to see what would happen."

In Honduras, the sunsets over the Caribbean Sea were so magnificent that when the last curve of the sun sank below the crystal clear waters an ethereal green light would flash across the horizon. In Sumatra, I skinny-dipped in jungle ponds filled with fresh rainwater while Thailand showed me Buddhism, meditation, and yoga. In the Philippines I swam with sharks and sea turtles, and Nepal and the Himalayas gave me a view from the top of the world. "What is my purpose in life?" and "Why am I here?" were the questions that echoed in my heart whether I was hitching a ride atop a beat-up old school bus or climbing up the side of a steaming volcano.

Yet as my search wore on, what I experienced out in the world were not answers—if anything I started forgetting the questions (and who wouldn't after spending three weeks doing little else other than dodging falling coconuts while lying on the beach). What I experienced was one large spiritual awakening, or more precisely, a series of spiritual awakenings.

Now, what I did not do was shave my head, buy a tambourine, and join the Hare Krishnas (though there was that opportunity once, in a bus station in Sydney), and I did not accept Jesus Christ into my life and become a born-again Christian (which had seemed the only option for far too long). No, my moment of rebirth, my new lease on life, came when I realized that I didn't have to wait until the end of the journey to get enlightened. As my globe-hopping had proved, I could achieve enlightenment *during* my search and not only that, I could achieve it dozens of times.

That realization has created the foundation of what you now hold in your hands. This book is a searcher's guide to enlightenment. In its pages you'll find practical instructions for achieving all things enlightening, whether that's firing up the car for a road trip to Montana, surfing waves off the coast of Australia, building a meditation platform in your backyard, or visiting an old-fashioned Baptist tent revival in the sticks. If it's organized religion you're after, you'll find the basics of all the world's major religions (as well as a few minor ones) along with prayer techniques, temple protocols, and instructions on how to build a shrine to your God, even if He happens to be Elvis. There's even a step-by-step guide on how to find your soul mate and instructions on what to do when that happens.

My journey around the world lasted seven years and the thing that I came to realize when it was over is that there is no one great enlightening moment in life except for the day you realize that life is a collection of enlightening moments, one unrelated to the next, but each equally as soulful. It reminds me of the story of poor Sisyphus rolling his rock up the mountain: Once he gets the rock to the top, it rolls down to the bottom, where he is doomed to start over, ad nauseam. He will never finish the job and see the fruits of his labor, so in order to find meaning in life, he has to find meaning in the actual rolling of the rock, in the journey to the top of the mountain. In the world, there are many different ways of telling the story of Sisyphus, but my favorite is in Tibet and Japan where the Buddhists say simply, the path is the goal. As far as I can tell, that means it's the search for life that is the meaning of life itself.

The pandit spoke first. "Piscine's piety is admirable. In these troubled times it's good to see a boy so keen on God. We all agree on that." The imam and the priest nodded. "But he can't be a Hindu, a Christian and a Muslim. It's impossible. He must choose."

"Hmmm, Piscine?" Mother nudged me. "How do you feel about the question?"

"Bapu Gandhi said, 'All religions are true.' I just want to love God," I blurted out, and looked down, red in the face.

— YANN MARTEL, *Life of Pi*

ONE

Practical Enlightenment

When most people think of enlightenment they think of church or temple, both of which have had a headlock on all things spiritual for centuries. But in the words of the great Peter Sellers, "not anymore." Now seekers are finding spirituality in dozens of imaginative new ways so that going to church—at least a traditional church—is actually getting in the way of many people's search. Having said that, organized religions that have been entrenched in world culture from day one aren't going anywhere. And indeed for those on the path to spiritual enlightenment, it might help to start with a look at some of the world's more practical belief systems. They have, after all, been in the business of saving souls for centuries and you might find a nugget of truth somewhere in the world's religions, especially if the only "spirituality" you've ever known has been your local Catholic chapel. You might even find that your God has quite a bit in common with someone else's. In fact, the practical path to enlightenment is really just about looking up from your small patch of world and having a closer look at a culture different from your own.

What to Do If God Appears to You

There is, perhaps, no bigger payoff, in terms of spiritual meaning, than witnessing the appearance of God. If this should happen to you, consider yourself lucky. Most people will live their entire lives without ever having come face-to-face with a higher power. And even when they do, the event is oftentimes so hair-raising that they simply keel over dead before getting to tell their friends. If you're one of the lucky ones and find yourself privy to a holy cameo—essentially the affirmation of the existence of a life beyond the mortal coil you presently call home—there are a few things you can do to keep from botching your moment of truth.

Steps to Enlightenment

1 ✆ Call Him or Her "Sir" or "Ma'am," whichever the case may be. "God" is also acceptable. "Hey you," "Holy Cow," or "You're not the boss of me" are not.

2 ✍ When God does appear to you, don't run. You will essentially be running from your own destiny. Besides, how can you run from God?

3 ✍ If God appears to you in the form of a burning bush, as He did to Moses on Mt. Sinai, don't panic and attempt to extinguish the flame. It will only hurt and you'll risk the real possibility of invoking the wrath of God, which is a surefire way to an entirely different kind of enlightenment.

4 ✍ Wearing sunglasses to shield your eyes from the blinding love and beauty of The Ultimate Truth is okay as long as the glasses aren't made with mirrored lenses, which might lead God to think you're an insolent nitwit.

5 ✍ After such an experience, you should know that most people will think you're bonkers if you start boasting about having just "seen God." It's best to consider yourself lucky, keep it under your hat, and live out your hereafter enlightened life with gusto. If you just have to share your experience—an understandable urge—know that sometimes it's better to speak by example than by words.

Word to the Wise

It's impossible to predict when God might appear to you, and it's very unlikely that you'll be able to arrange for an appearance by the Almighty (this is not about who you know and networking at cocktail parties). However, your chances of having a private encounter with a higher power increase with the more open you are to the possibility of seeing a deity. In fact, those who are actively searching for God (whether in the dappled yellow sunlight of a Caribbean palm tree or in the mystic poetry of Rumi) have been known to see Him more frequently than those who aren't.

Mainstream Religion

For each difference that you can find in the various religions around the world there is a similarity. In fact, it may be that all roads lead to one place: enlightenment. For something totally different, try mixing and matching religions to find a way that works for your personal path.

Note: the terms CE and BCE—Common Era and Before Common Era—are used instead of AD and BC—Anno Domini, which is Latin for the Year of Our Lord, and Before Christ. The numbered dates are the same (i.e., 2004 CE is the same as 2004 AD). This is because most of the world isn't Christian and doesn't consider Jesus Christ all that important.

Hinduism

If you don't know much about the Hindu religion, then buckle your seat belt. It claims more gods than there are people in the United States as well as an intricate series of rituals and festivities. It's also the world's oldest religion.

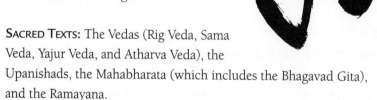

Sacred Texts: The Vedas (Rig Veda, Sama Veda, Yajur Veda, and Atharva Veda), the Upanishads, the Mahabharata (which includes the Bhagavad Gita), and the Ramayana.

Age: Founded in 1500 BCE, making it the world's oldest organized religion.

Followers: 762 million, the world's third largest.

GEOGRAPHIC LOCATION: The majority of practicing Hindus live in India, Nepal, and Sri Lanka, although nearly two million people practice Hinduism in North America.

LIFE AFTER DEATH: Transmigration of the soul (also known as reincarnation) over many lifetimes, though it is possible to escape this pattern and achieve total enlightenment after living several lifetimes of pure and devotional acts and thoughts. Some Hindus believe that after one achieves total enlightenment, they go to one of seven heavens (depending on which god they followed during their many lives). It's also possible to have a brief stopover in one of these heavens after a life of particularly good karma. Once the karma is "used up" though, they have to leave and get on with the next life.

BELIEFS: Hindus believe that because they will die and then be reborn into another life (a cycle known as samsara), what they do and how they act in their present life determines who or what they will become in their next life (those who do particularly bad things can come back as animals, which is a major setback). A person's good and bad deeds are known as karma and generally speaking if you have good karma in this life, you'll get a better life next time around. In general, the four aims of all Hindus are dharma, or religious devotion, *artha*, or economic and marital prosperity, *kama*, or sensual, sexual, and intellectual enjoyment, and *moksha*, or liberation from the cycle of reincarnation, which is also referred to as self-realization.

GODS: Brahman is, in theory, the one supreme God in the Hindu religion, but Hindus believe that Brahman has manifested itself in many different ways. The three most important manifestations of Brahman are Brahma, Vishnu, and Shiva. (See Hindu God Primer, page 6.)

Sects or Denominations: A large majority of Hindus consider themselves Vaishnavites and worship Lord Vishnu. Shaivism, whose followers worship Lord Shiva, is another major denomination. The Hare Krishna and Sikh religions began as Hindu sects.

Prayers and Practices: Meditation and yoga, daily devotions or prayers, and daily public rituals such as *puja*.

Hindu God Primer

"Truth is one, and the learned call it by many names."

—Hindu saying from the Rig Veda

At last count there were 330 million gods and goddesses in the Hindu religion. That number again is *three hundred and thirty million.* Talk about omnipresent! Basically, there's a deity for every conceivable malfunction, pleasure, pain, and success in the vast human range of experience. The list below represents only the most popular gods and goddesses.

Major Hindu Gods

Brahman is the supreme God in the Hindu religion but Hindus believe that He has manifested Himself in millions of ways. The three most important manifestations of Brahman make up a Hindu triad know as the Trimurti. They are Brahma, the creator, Vishnu, the preserver, and Shiva, the destroyer.

Brahma, the Creator God, has four heads and four hands and is often incarnated as a swan, which in the Hindu religion is known for its ability to judge between good and bad. Lord Brahma is said to have created the meditative mantra OM. (See Chanting the OM, page 31.)

VISHNU, the Preserver God, is believed to be responsible for balancing good and evil in the universe. Also, Hindus believe that Vishnu will be reincarnated on the earth ten times, nine of which have already occurred. Krishna, one of the most popular Hindu gods, is the eighth incarnation of Vishnu. Buddha is the ninth. Lord Vishnu is often depicted as having blue skin and four arms, while sitting on top of a serpent.

SHIVA, the Destroyer God, is also the god of regeneration and reproduction and because of that is often worshipped in the form of a penis. Yes, a penis. Normally, though, Shiva is depicted in a calm, sitting posture with long flowing hair and a serpent around his neck. In one of his hands, he holds a trident.

Other Popular Gods

KRISHNA is the eighth reincarnation of Vishnu and is believed to have lived anywhere from 1471 BCE to 5571 BCE. He is often depicted as a handsome young man with long flowing dark hair who is playing the flute. In addition to His divine origins, Krishna is believed to have been quite a hero as well as a ladies' man. He is said to have killed numerous dragons and monsters and legend has it that He had sixteen thousand wives. The Bhagavad Gita, which is the sixth book of the sacred Hindu text, the Mahabharata, contains the teachings and life history of Krishna.

GANESH is the oldest son of Lord Shiva and the Goddess Parvati. He has the head of an elephant, four hands, and a large belly. Ganesh is often invoked at the start of a performance or venture because he is considered the god who removes obstacles. Like many Hindu gods and goddesses he has several names: Ganapati, Gajanana, and Vigneshwara.

RAMA is the seventh incarnation of Lord Vishnu and is the hero of the epic Hindu poem the Ramayana, a love story with moral and spiritual themes. In that story, Rama is depicted as the ideal son, husband, and king. He is often depicted with His wife, Sita, His brother, Lakshman, and the monkey god Hanuman, and He is usually holding a bow and arrow, a weapon with which He destroys evil.

Hanuman, the monkey god, is also a hero of the Ramayana and is Lord Rama's sidekick. He is said to embody courage, bravery, hope, knowledge, intelligence, and devotion. Like Ganesh, Hanuman has many names, including Mahaveera, Pavan-suta, and Bajarangbali.

Some Hindu Goddesses

SARASWATI is the wife of Lord Brahma and is known as the goddess of learning, music, and fine arts. She is usually depicted with four hands, two of which are playing a guitar-like instrument known as a vina, and She is often seen sitting atop a swan. In India, She is honored once a year with the Saraswati Puja festival, a day in which all walks of life pray for a fruitful upcoming year.

LAKSHMI is married to Lord Vishnu and is the goddess of spiritual and material wealth. She is depicted as a beautiful woman and is either standing or sitting on a lotus flower. Usually, when Vishnu was reincarnated, Lakshmi was reincarnated with him—She is Sita, Rama's wife in the Ramayana, as well as Rukmini, Krishna's wife. There are many festivals in India that are held to invoke her blessings, especially among businessmen.

PARVATI is the wife of Lord Shiva and the mother of Lord Ganesh and is the Mother Goddess as well as the goddess of protection and married life. She commonly takes on three forms, depending on what mood she's in. Paravati is depicted as a calm, loving mother and wife, and when She is mad or feeling protective She becomes Durga or Kali, both of whom have eight arms and carry lots of weapons. As Durga she rides a tiger, and as Kali she stands atop a dead body.

Temple Protocol—Hindu Temples

If you want to check out how the Hindus worship (or just see the inside of a very interesting piece of architecture), you can't just walk in willy-nilly and plop down in the nearest church pew. For one thing, there are no church pews. For another, you need to bring a small gift of food. And remember, a can of SpaghettiOs is not cool. Bring rice or something that doesn't require a can opener.

The Hindu religion places a lot of importance on sacred sites (of which there are thousands in India) and usually temples are places next to bodies of water to symbolize how upon entering a temple, an individual cleanses him or herself. The water is also a place where worshipers actually do take a dip and cleanse themselves before entering the holy site. Where there is no river, lake, or ocean, a temple will have a pool of water or a fountain of some kind for just this purpose.

Also, when you walk up to a Hindu temple or temple compound you'll notice scads of shoes outside the front entrance. They are not part of a fund-raiser or temple clearance sale. Before you go in remove your shoes (and remember where you put them). When you come out, don't give in to the urge to slip on somebody else's fine leather sandals. Shiva is watching!

Inside a temple, there will be several different areas of worship. Variations on these will be found at any Hindu temple around the world. There's the main shrine room, a statue of Nandi the bull, a secondary shrine, and one or more memorial shrines.

Steps to Enlightenment

1 ✿ First off, strip down to your undies and take a dip in the temple fountain, pool, or river. If no one else is doing this, then consider just washing your hands and feet.

2 ✿ Next, go to the main shrine. Here you'll find any number of deities along with a variety of offerings or *prasad*. It is here where you can leave a gift or food offering yourself. If a priest is there, sit on the floor while the priest performs the puja ritual of waking, bathing, dressing, feeding, and putting to bed an image of the deity or deities. (No, I'm not making this up.) After the ritual, the priest will pass out the *prasad* to the visitors.

3 ✿ After partaking of the *prasad* or leaving your offering, head over to the statue of Nandi. This bull was Shiva's personal attendant (if there is no statue of Nandi, you will most likely not be in a temple devoted to Shiva). He is also a symbol for fatherhood and strength. Here you can sit and meditate on those two manly things or you can just pay your respects and head over to the secondary shrine.

4 ✿ At the secondary shrine you'll find a statue of either Shiva or Vishnu, depending on who is worshiped in the main shrine (the other will be found here). It's possible there is a statue of a female goddess, usually the wife of the main shrine god, or of Hanuman or Ganesh (for detailed explanations of Hindu Gods, see Hindu God Primer, page 6). Leave another gift for the *prasad*.

5 ✿ Lastly, cruise by one of the memorial shrines and have a moment of silence for the saint that is interred in these shrines. Hindus normally believe in cremation, but the bodies of inspirational individuals are kept preserved.

Word to the Wise

If you walk into a temple where Vishnu is worshiped, often there will be a container full of basil. It doesn't hurt to bring along a sprig to offer.

Christianity

It pervades much of Western culture, so we might as well review some of the facts. At least you'll know what you're talking about the next time you say church is boring.

SACRED TEXTS: The Bible (The Old and New Testaments).

AGE: Founded in 70 CE, a few decades after the death of Jesus.

FOLLOWERS: Two billion, making this the world's largest religion.

GEOGRAPHIC LOCATION: Christianity, in one form or another, is the majority religion in North and South America, Europe, Russia, Australia, New Zealand, and the lower half of Africa.

LIFE AFTER DEATH: The belief is that life continues after death either in heaven or hell, depending on how one has led their life. Some Christians believe in a Judgment Day, similar to the Islamic belief, in which God will judge all souls before they are allowed entrance into heaven or they are cast into hell.

BELIEFS: Christians believe that Jesus came to earth as the divinely conceived Son of God and died by crucifixion on the cross after being sentenced to death by the Roman governor Pontius Pilate. They also believe that Jesus rose from the dead on the Sunday after his death (this day is now known as Easter) and ascended to heaven. His death represents for Christians an atonement for all human wrongdoings (or sins) and therefore if an individual accepts Jesus as the Savior of humankind and repents his or her sins, he or she will be forgiven by God.

Otherwise, since there is such a wide range of Christian denominations (see below), it's hard to quantify any singular Christian creed to live by. However, the three main virtues that all Christians accept are faith, hope, and love.

GODS: Christians believe in one all-powerful deity, God. However, they also believe that God comes in two other forms: the Holy Spirit and Jesus, who was both human and divine as "the son of God." All three together form the Holy Trinity: God the Father, God the Son, and God the Holy Spirit. This Trinity promotes the notion that God is "one-in-three and three-in-one."

SECTS OR DENOMINATIONS: After Jesus died in 33 CE, his followers regrouped in Jerusalem into three distinct groups: Jewish Christians, who viewed Jesus as a prophet but not a deity; Pauline Christians, who considered Jesus's teachings as the "Word of God"; and Gnostic Christians, who believe in the divine power of knowledge rather than faith.

There are literally thousands of different Christian denominations in the world today (one source says there are 1,200 in the United States alone) ranging from Catholic to Jehovah's Witness to Amish. Many of the groups have widely differing views of the religion. Some are far more tolerant than others and issues like homosexuality, abortion, and female ordination continue to split groups even further.

Roman Catholicism is the largest denomination of Christianity and they believe that the pope is the leader of the church. The two other main groups are Eastern Orthodoxy, which is similar to Catholicism but does not believe in a single leader, and Protestantism, which came about after Martin Luther defiantly nailed his ninety-five theses to a German church door in 1517. His protest (hence the term Protestant), created a very diverse group that rejects the pope as its leader and believes in a more active and equal role of its followers.

PRAYERS AND PRACTICES: Most Christians meet for prayers and singing each Sunday at a church or cathedral. Many churches also hold a communion (also known as the Eucharist, Mass, and the Lord's Supper), in which a priest or minister passes out food and wine (usually in the form of communion wafers and grape juice) to the congregation to celebrate the death and resurrection of Jesus.

Buddhism

Buddhists don't actually consider Buddhism a religion as much as a way of life. It has a lot in common with Hinduism, just without the gods (never mind ex-*American Gigolo* Richard Gere, who could be the most famous Buddhist next to the Dalai Lama). The Dalai Lama, by the way, is considered to be one of two religious and administrative leaders of Tibet; the other is the Panchen Lama. The term Dalai Lama means "Ocean of Wisdom" and he is considered a reincarnation of his predecessor all the way back to the first Dalai Lama, Sonam Gyatso, who lived in the late sixteenth century. The present Dalai Lama is number fourteen and he lives in exile in India. His official name is Jetsun Jamphel Ngawang Lobsang Yeshe Tenzin Gyatso, which is "Holy Lord, Gentle Glory, Compassionate, Defender of the Faith, Ocean of Wisdom" in English. Tibetans affectionately refer to His Holiness as *Yeshe Norbu,* the "Wish-Fulfilling Gem" or sometimes just *Kundun,* "The Presence."

Buddhism got its start when a man named Siddhartha Gautama, a king's son, decided to venture out beyond the walls of his father's house and experience life. At first he became an ascetic, denying all material possessions and earthly needs, including food. Legend has it that he almost died from starvation before seeing the light and realizing that extreme measures are not the way to enlightenment. Instead, he began practicing everything in moderation and he started practicing meditation. He called his way of life the Middle Way. After teaching his ideas to a small group of followers, Siddhartha gained total enlightenment in 535 BCE while sitting beneath a bodhi tree. He was in his early thirties. It was then he took the name Lord Buddha. He died in 483 BCE.

SACRED TEXTS: The main text of Buddha's teachings can be found in the Tripitaka, which was written by some Buddhist monks more than two hundred years after Siddhartha Gautama's death.

AGE: Buddha lived in the fifth and sixth century BCE, making Buddhism about 2,500 years old.

FOLLOWERS: Some records show that Buddhism is the third largest religious group in the United States, with three to four million followers. It has the fourth largest following in the world. Only Christianity, Islam, and Hinduism claim more devotees.

GEOGRAPHIC LOCATION: Buddhism is overwhelmingly the number one choice of religion in Thailand, Laos, Cambodia, Burma, Korea, and Japan. Unofficially, China also has very large Buddhist communities (especially the Chinese province of Tibet, just north of Nepal). Buddhism claims ever increasing numbers of followers in Europe and North America, where there are a series of Buddhist monasteries and practicing monks from around the world.

LIFE AFTER DEATH: Like the Hindus, Buddhists believe in reincarnation. The soul has to live through many cycles of birth, living, and death while trying to renounce desire and the self, which they believe is the way to total enlightenment. Once they achieve this, they can go to nirvana, which is a state of liberation and freedom from suffering.

BELIEFS: The main Buddhist mantra is that all life is suffering and that only by following a set of rules established by the Buddha can one free oneself from that suffering. That idea is set out in the Four Noble Truths:

1 ☯ *Dukkha:* Life is suffering and there are many causes of suffering including pain, failure, sickness, and death.

2 ☯ *Samudaya:* The cause of suffering is desire.

3 ☯ *Nirodha:* One can free oneself from suffering by reaching a state of total nonattachment, which is nirvana.

4 ✿ *Magga:* The path to nirvana is set out in the Eightfold Path, which is a set of virtues to live by.

Other rules include the Five Precepts:

1 ✿ Do not kill or harm.

2 ✿ Do not steal.

3 ✿ Do not lie.

4 ✿ Do not misuse sex, which means no adultery or sexual harassment (monks and nuns take a vow of celibacy).

5 ✿ Do not consume drugs or alcohol or do anything that clouds the mind.

For Buddhists, mental preparation is the key to enlightenment, so by meditating one can control and sharpen the mind to bring about a higher state of consciousness.

GODS: None. The Buddhist faith is a faith in life itself and those that follow this path do so with a set of life rules to live by rather than by worshiping a god.

SECTS OR DENOMINATIONS: The three main branches of Buddhism are Theravada or Southern Buddhism, which is what you'll find in Southeast Asia; Mahayana or Northern Buddhism, which is practiced in China, Japan, Korea, and Mongolia; and Tibetan Buddhism, which is given its own brand of the Buddhist faith because of how isolated Tibet is from the rest of the world.

In the past one hundred years or so there has been a strong movement toward a kind of Buddhism that has a greater relevance for Western cultures. This type of Buddhism is sometimes referred to as

Modern Buddhism. British writer and Buddhist Alan Watts and Buddhist monk Shunryu Suzuki are often attributed with making large contributions to this particular brand of Buddhism.

PRAYERS AND PRACTICES: Buddhists do a lot of meditating. They also kneel and give respect to images and statues of the Buddha as well as to the bodhi trees found in Southern and Southeast Asia. However, there is no prayer, per se. Chanting is also big in the Buddhist faith, as Buddhists believe it helps clarify the mind and clear away desires.

How to Become a Buddha

> *"The only difference between a Buddha and an ordinary man
> is that one realizes it and the other doesn't."*

—Buddhist Monk Hui Neng

Becoming a Buddha (literally an "awakened one") is another way of saying you have become enlightened about the truth of human existence (the dharma). With that bit of handy knowledge, you can then be excused from the cycle of life, death, and rebirth, meaning you no longer have to live life over again trying to right the wrongs of your previous existence. Finally, some peace and quiet!

Siddhartha Gautama, the Shakyamuni Buddha, did it in Northern India and present day Nepal in the fifth and sixth centuries BCE by practicing what he called the Middle Way, which is a way of living that avoids extremes. Avoid too much self-indulgence, he said, but don't deny yourself either. Luckily, he left instructions on exactly how to live one's life by the Middle Way (it's easier said than done). These instructions are written down as the Eightfold Path. For us to become Buddhas too, we're going to have to go that route.

The Eightfold Path

1 ✿ Right Views. The first of the eight steps on the way to nirvana instructs Buddhas-in-waiting to know and understand the Four Noble Truths. They are 1) suffering exists, 2) there is a reason for suffering, 3) there is a way to end suffering and 4) the way to end suffering is through the Eightfold Path.

2 ✿ Right Thoughts. This one is a toughie, but no one said becoming totally enlightened was going to be easy. The second of the eight steps is letting go of want and desire. Buddha learned that desire and want only increase suffering, which gets in the way of the dharma. This is the reason many Buddhists become monks, shave their heads, and remove themselves from the world; it's less tempting. Also, having right thoughts is to act with kindness and avoid hurting anything, even giant cockroaches (which could be you in the next life).

3 ✿ Right Speech. To be a Buddha you have to tell the truth, dispense wisdom, and avoid speaking bad about others (even your boss).

4 ✿ Right Action. Don't steal or cheat. This is just standard practice for most things in life.

5 ✿ Right Livelihood. Number five on the list basically recognizes the fact that we all have to pay our rent. The catch is that the jobs we take or the ways in which we earn money shouldn't hurt other people or cause bloodshed. This one might also be somewhat difficult, especially in bad economies when you have to make a living doing something, even if it's working for Lockheed Martin or McDonald's, both of which have been known to produce products that harm others.

6 ✿ Right Effort. As we get far along the path, it's important to stay positive and encourage each other to stick to the Eightfold Path.

7 ✺ Right Mindfulness. Number seven is going to take patience and there's going to be lots of mistakes before we can get it right. Basically, right mindfulness is a way in which we avoid having actions or thoughts that might affect the world (either now or in the future) in a negative way. Doesn't it seem like most politicians are out of luck on this whole nirvana thing?

8 ✺ Right Concentration. The only thing you can do for this step in the path is do the other steps first, for once we follow the Eightfold Path, we will have the right kind of concentration to become Buddhas.

How to Beg for Alms

While necessary for the soul and the spiritual quest, years of searching can both work up an appetite and empty a person's bank account. Fortunately, begging for food—or to use a more monk-like term, begging for alms—is a perfectly good option and a really affordable one at that. In fact, it doesn't cost anything at all, save for the initial start-up costs of getting a container to hold all the goodies friendly passersby might be so kind as to help you out with.

The best part about begging, though, is that it, too, is a great way to enlightenment, if only because you will understand what it means to be a Buddhist monk and have no material possessions whatsoever, not even a box of macaroni and cheese. In the Buddhist tradition, especially in Thailand, monks go out from the monasteries each morning to collect food for their daily meal, which they only have one of and which must be eaten before 1 P.M. each day. The reason for this alms ceremony is twofold: It allows the monks to eat without compromising their oath of not keeping any material possessions or killing any living thing (including plants); and it allows the giver of alms to earn some good karma.

You Will Need:

An alms bowl with a lid
Three hours or so before noon every day
Buddhist monk's robe
A few understanding people who are familiar with the
    Buddhist tradition of begging for alms

Steps to Enlightenment

1 ✪ The first step is to plan your route. Simply wandering through the streets never got anyone a decent meal. Figure out what you need to fill you up and then determine how many houses you need to get food from. It always helps to plan in a circular route (remember to go clockwise) so that you can end up where you started from (and dig right in).

2 ✪ Next, go along the route and explain to the residents what you're planning. This is especially important if you're planning on going out for alms in a predominantly Christian society that might not understand what the heck you're doing at their front door, barefoot, enrobed, and waiting for last night's leftovers. Definitely let them know what *they* have to gain (i.e., good karma) by feeding you, a monk of the highest Buddhist order.

3 ✪ Tell everyone what time you'll come by (9:00 A.M.) and explain to them that like the alms ceremony in Thailand, they'll need to stand outside their homes to wait for your approach at the appointed hour.

4 ✪ When it's time to leave, put on your robe. Don't forget the alms bowl and its lid!

5 ✪ Approach the first person (who should be waiting with his or her offering out by the curb). When they offer the food, take the lid off

your alms container and let them put the food in it. It's important to know that a Buddhist monk cannot accept an offering by hand.

6 ✪ After the offering is made, some givers may thank you for allowing them to better their lot in life by boosting their karma. Let them. Then you may smile out of thanks. Words on your part are not necessary.

7 ✪ Once you have finished your rounds, head home, but do not eat until you get inside.

Word to the Wise

If going out for alms is nerve-racking or if it gives you doubt about the right path to enlightenment, try to calm your mind by watching the doubt come and go. Consider the alms as a simple walk around the neighborhood to see what there is to see. You are going out with nothing but who you are and you shall return with nothing but yourself.

Temple Protocol—Buddhism

Buddhist temples are called stupas, which is the Sanskrit word for burial mound. Buddha told his followers to cremate his body and bury the ashes in a series of stupas, which would in turn serve as destinations for meditation and Buddhist prayer.

These days, stupas are far more elaborate than simple burial mounds. They are more like enormous Hershey's Kisses with elongated pointy tops, but painted white. These sit on a square base upon which is painted sets of eyes looking in each direction to symbolize the omnipresent eyes of the Buddha.

Buddhist temples are almost always surrounded by a wall and inside they house gargantuan statues of Buddha in several different poses (reclining, sitting in the lotus position, etc.) as well as a number of ritual shrines where visitors make offerings, spin prayer wheels, light candles, and ring bells.

Steps to Enlightenment

1 ✿ Remove the shoes. No, they won't get ripped off. It's bad karma to do that sort of thing.

2 ✿ Upon entering the temple, go to one of several small Buddha statues and shrines inside the temple where you will find a small cup inside a bucket or basin of water. Dip and pour a cup of water over the statue's head to cleanse it.

3 ✿ Here you will also light incense or candles and leave a food offering on the shrine.

4 ✿ Next, walk clockwise around the stupa. This circle symbolizes the Wheel of Life or the endless cycle of life, death, and rebirth (the Buddha, of course, made it out of this cycle and if you follow his path you will, too!).

5 ✿ Along the circle there will be prayer wheels embedded into the wall of the temple. On each wheel a prayer or mantra is painted. Spin each one in a clockwise motion as you pass it to repeat the mantra and send the prayers out into the world.

6 ✿ Also, if there are any small bells, ring them lightly one time on your way around the temple.

Islam

Islam's getting a bad rap as of late, what with some of its followers blowing themselves and others up in the name of Allah— an odd interpretation of the Koran if you ask me. Islam in Arabic means "to submit to the will of God" and a Muslim is "one who submits to the will of God." For most practicing Muslims, the Islamic religion is a peace-loving belief with some beautiful life philosophies. Anyone interested in Islam will find plenty of opportunity for total enlightenment.

SACRED TEXTS: The Qur'an, also known as the Koran. The Hadith is a companion guide to the life examples of the Islamic prophet Muhammad.

AGE: Founded in 622 CE when Muhammad relocated to Medina after getting the boot from Mecca. The journey from Mecca to Medina is known as the Hijrah or Hegira. This journey also marks the start of the Islamic calendar, or 1 AH (After Hijrah).

FOLLOWERS: Between 700 million and 1.2 billion, making it the world's second-largest religion (after Christianity).

GEOGRAPHIC LOCATION: Over 90 percent of the population of the Middle East, North Africa, and Indonesia practice Islam. It is also the majority religion in most of West Africa and has substantial followers in East Africa, Eastern Europe, India, Surinam (in South America), and parts of the old Soviet Union. Some estimates have seven million people practicing Islam in the United States.

LIFE AFTER DEATH: Muslims believe that after the body dies, the soul waits in the grave until the end of the world or Judgment Day. At this time, all souls are resurrected from the dead and those who believed in and practiced the Five Pillars of Islam during their lives go to heaven or Paradise. Those who didn't go to hell or the Fire.

BELIEFS: Muslims believe that God handed down divine revelations to several Prophets, including Adam, Abraham, Moses, and Jesus. However, they believe that God's final revelation was to the Prophet Muhammad over a twenty-three-year period from 610 to 632 CE. The revelations received by Muhammad became the Koran. Muslims believe that there is one God—Allah—and that He offers eternal salvation in heaven to those who believe in Him and follow the rules of conduct set out in the Koran. All Muslims strive to achieve the Five Pillars of Islam: Declaring daily faith to God and His Prophet Muhammad; five daily prayers; a month of fasting every nine months (a time called Ramadan); giving money to the needy; and making a pilgrimage (a Hajj) to Mecca at least once.

GODS AND PROPHETS: Allah (Arabic for "God") is the unequaled creator and ruler of the universe. Muhammad is the Messenger of God.

SECTS OR DENOMINATIONS: After Muhammad's death in the mid seventh century, leadership in the Islamic religion was held by caliphs or deputies who were chosen from Muhammad's tribe. A split occurred almost immediately because one group thought Ali ibn Abi Talib, Muhammad's son-in-law by marriage to his daughter Fatima, should be caliph and that all future caliphs should be direct descendants of Muhammad, while another group thought Abu Bakr, one of Muhammad's close followers, was the rightful heir to the caliphate and that future caliphs should be democratically elected. Those who supported Ali called themselves Shiites and those who supported Abu became known as Sunni. Today more than 80 percent of Muslims are Sunni.

Sufism is another sect that arose out of Islam. It practices a more mystical form of the religion. The Whirling Dervishes of Turkey is a Sufi order. Rumi is one of the greatest Sufi poets.

PRAYERS AND PRACTICES: Prayers five times a day and gathering at a mosque for Friday midday prayers.

Judaism

Considering all the persecution the Jewish people have endured over the years and all the trouble that surrounds their small country in the Middle East, the Jewish religion claims a relatively small number of followers.

SACRED TEXTS: The Tanakh (known as the Old Testament to Christians), which is separated by Jews into three parts: the Torah, the Nevi'im, and the Ketuvim. The Talmud is also considered sacred. It is a collection of Jewish laws, medical writings, and moral stories.

AGE: Some Jews trace the origin of their religion to 2000 BCE and Abraham, though others say Judaism started with the kingdom of Saul in the tenth or eleventh century BCE.

FOLLOWERS: Eighteen million people worldwide.

Geographic Location: The Jewish religion can be found in many parts of Western and Eastern Europe as well as in Russia and the former Soviet states, but most followers live in North America and Israel.

Life After Death: Like Christians and Muslims, Jews believe that a person's soul goes to heaven after death to live forever. Unlike Christians and Muslims, however, Jews will not burn in the fiery pits of hell for all eternity. The Jewish hell, which is sometimes referred to as Gehinnom, is more like a purgatory where unsavory souls are cleansed before being reunited with God.

Beliefs: In medieval times, a Jewish scholar and rabbi named Moshe ben Maimon, also known as Maimonides, wrote a concise list of Jewish beliefs known as the Thirteen Principles. The Jewish people still consider most of these to be accurate. They are:

1 ✪ God exists.

2 ✪ God is one and unique.

3 ✪ God is incorporeal.

4 ✪ God is eternal.

5 ✪ Prayer is to be directed to God alone and to no other.

6 ✪ The words of the prophets are true.

7 ✪ Moses was the greatest of the prophets, and his prophecies are true.

8 ✪ The Written Torah and Oral Torah (most of which is in the Talmud) were given to Moses.

9 ✿ There will be no other Torah.

10 ✿ God knows the thoughts and deeds of men.

11 ✿ God will reward the good and punish the wicked.

12 ✿ The Messiah will come.

13 ✿ The dead will be resurrected.

GODS: Followers of Judaism believe in one all-powerful God who divinely inspired three patriarchs: Abraham, Isaac, and Jacob. God also handed Jewish law down to Moses. In all Jewish texts the term God is usually spelled G-d because it is forbidden to write His name in full.

SECTS OR DENOMINATIONS: The three most popular Jewish movements are Orthodox Judaism, Conservative Judaism, and Reform Judaism. Orthodox is the oldest and most conservative of the group and those who practice this form of Judaism do so as it has been practiced for centuries, including eating the right foods and wearing specific clothes and hairstyles. Conservative Judaism is, go figure, a little less conservative than Orthodox, while Reform Judaism is the most liberal of the three. Most Jews living in the United States are Reform Jews. They believe in the basic tenets of Judaism but they are not required to follow traditional laws.

PRAYERS AND PRACTICES: Reform Jews practice weekly rest and worship at a synagogue on the Sabbath, which starts at sundown on Friday and ends at sundown on Saturday. Orthodox Jews, on the other hand, have three very involved prayers a day, the first one of which lasts forty-five minutes. On the Sabbath, they pray four times. So much for the rest.

Prayer Techniques

"Prayer does not change God, but it changes him who prays."

—Søren Kierkegaard

All organized religions recommend ways in which to ritually connect with your God or, in the case of Buddhism, a way in which to connect with your true self (which may be your God). Instead of switching Gods, it might be a fun experiment to just keep your God and just switch the way you pray. For total enlightenment, try out a different technique every day for a week.

Hinduism

Hindus don't pray as much as they offer devotion to their various deities. *Bhakti* is what followers of this religion call their exchanges with their gods and goddesses. This is done by chanting, singing, playing music, and dancing. *Puja* is another form of devotion in which individuals or families set up shrines to their gods. These shrines hold images of the god and goddess as well as flowers, food, incense, and candles. Every day, Hindus perform *puja* by offering food and flowers at the shrine, lighting the candles and incense, and tasting the food at the end of the ritual. All of the senses are experienced during a *puja*.

You Will Need:

A shrine
Images of your god(s)
Bowls of water
Cooked rice
Ghee (butter oil that has been separated from its milk)

Sugar and fruit

Incense

Candles (optional: candle lamp)

Steps to Enlightenment

1 ↺ Approach your shrine (for instructions on making a Hindu shrine, turn to page 50) and symbolically and politely offer your God a seat ("Please, take a load off" works just fine).

2 ↺ Next, symbolically bathe your God, clothe him or her in crisp clean clothes, rub on a nice perfume or scented oil, and consider an accessory such as a new bead necklace. Flowers are always a nice thing to give, especially if God has had a trying day. Just lay them worshipfully at His or Her feet. (The idea here is not to play a spiritual game of dolls; Hindus do these things to cultivate an emotional and sensory relationship with the divine.)

3 ↺ After the deity has been tidied up and is smelling nice, light some incense and a candle or candle lamp. Pass the candle or lamp in front of the God. This is again another way of experiencing the senses with the divine.

4 ↺ Place a new food offering of rice, fruit, butter, and sugar. Also, refill the water bowls at the shrine.

5 ↺ Bow once before the God and the offering. This symbolizes that the food and water have been blessed.

6 ↺ Take a few sips of water and eat a modest portion of the food from the newly blessed offering.

Word to the Wise

If you're actually in India while performing *puja*, use bottled water at the shrine. Blessed or not, the stuff out of the tap will give you the runs.

Christianity

Put on your pajamas, then before you get in bed, kneel down, put your palms together, close your eyes and . . . ask God for a new Mercedes. Okay, so maybe that's not how it works in every Christian household. The fact is, there are so many different ways to pray—from reciting Hail Marys in a church pew to clasping hands around the dinner table—that there is no right or wrong way to do it. In fact, prayer is often used as a simple form of meditation. By intently focusing on something you can clear the mind and give yourself a much-needed respite from the stresses of daily life. What could be more spiritual than that?

You Will Need:

A quiet place

Steps to Enlightenment

1 ✿ Sit with your eyes closed and focus your mind on what you wish to pray for. This could be for peace in the world. You might want to send some good vibes to a friend who's going through a rough patch. Whatever you decide, think about that and empty the mind of everything else.

2 ✿ Further focus your thoughts by whispering or speaking the words you are thinking.

3 ✺ Repeat these steps for about five minutes as many times a day as you feel necessary, though if your boss catches you doing this once at work, suspend any prayer until you get home or at least until you get outside to smoke a cigarette. Praying while in the drive-through line at a fast-food restaurant is similarly frowned upon by those persons in line behind you.

Buddhism

The main form of prayer for Buddhists is meditation and this is done on a daily basis while sitting cross-legged in a quiet place for as little as five minutes and as much as an hour (see Clear the Mind: Simple Meditation Techniques, page 59). Also, Buddhists do lots of chanting in low guttural voices and in some places this is considered more important than meditation. The most famous chant is *Om Mane Padme Hum* (pronounced AH-owm MAH-nay PAHD-may HOOM), which means "My heart is the jewel in the lotus," the jewel being Buddha or the enlightened mind.

Steps to Enlightenment

Chanting the OM

1 ✺ Sit down in a quiet place as if to meditate, then close your eyes and begin saying the mantra slowly and deliberately. Your voice should come from the bottom of the throat, in as deep a baritone as you can comfortably manage, almost as if you are speaking from your chest.

2 ✺ As you slowly say each word, begin to focus on the vibrations. Your voice shouldn't be too loud, nor too soft. Don't change inflections with each word. Just say them in the same tone as if all the words are becoming one word.

3 ✪ Breathe in after completing the entire mantra and breathe out slowly as you say the words over again. Your breath and the vibrations of your voice begin to become one.

4 ✪ Think of a jewel at the center of the lotus flower and imagine freedom from suffering. Say the words, feel the vibrations. Imagine the full blossoming lotus flower is your heart, blooming in your chest as you say the words and feel the vibrations. Imagine compassion for all beings as you chant. The jewel is the clear, calm center of your consciousness.

Islam

There are many different kinds of prayers in the Islamic religion, but the one that all Muslims partake in is the *salat,* or the five daily prayers. These are done at dawn, midday, afternoon, sunset, and evening (you can pick up a timetable with exact prayer times at your local Islamic mosque). These prayers can take place anywhere and they can be done solo or with a group (though the latter is always encouraged). It's important that the individual doing the praying face in the direction of the holy city of Mecca. You don't need a satellite positioning device. A general direction will do fine. If you don't know where Mecca is, well, just go for it this one time and get your hands on a map before the next prayer (it's in Saudi Arabia, which is in the Middle East, which is generally northeast of the United States).

You Will Need:

A prayer mat (a yoga mat will do in a pinch, a towel in a real pinch).
A bucket of water or nearby sink for washing the face, hands, and feet.
Space enough to stand up, put your hands over your head, kneel
    down, and bend over forward.
About fifteen minutes.

Steps to Enlightenment

1 ✪ Before each prayer it's important to do a ritual cleansing of the face, hands and feet known as the *wudu*. This purifies the body and prepares the mind for the task at hand.

2 ✪ Stand facing toward Mecca and lay out your mat in front of you.

3 ✪ Lift your hands up so that they are basically on each side of your face and say, "God is great."

4 ✪ Bring your hands down in front of your chest, palms up and say, "Glory and praise be to God, blessed is Your name, There is no God but You."

5 ✪ Bend at the waist with hands on your legs and the eyes looking down at the ground and say, "God is great."

6 ✪ Kneel down on your mat and place your forehead on the mat in front of you. Your hands should be flat on the ground. Say, "Glory to God."

7 ✪ Bring your body upright but stay kneeling and say, "God is Great."

8 ✪ Repeat steps six and seven three times and when you come back to kneeling on the third time, say, "Peace and mercy of God be on you."

Judaism

For Orthodox and seriously committed male Jews, prayer should happen three times a day in the morning, afternoon, and evening each weekday. On the Jewish Sabbath—Saturdays—four prayers are required. If you're a woman, you can breathe a sigh of relief: Jewish women only have to pray once a day during the week, preferably in the morning.

As for what a person prays for or about, it used to be left up to the individual but everyone kept asking for things like a new iPod or a daughter who, "please Lord," would decide against going to cosmetology school. So in the mid-1st Century CE, the Rabbis and other temple folk decided to create some standardized prayers. It took a while for them to write it all down, but at the end of the 9th Century they came up with the Siddur, which is a book of prayers. Since then dozens of siddurim (the plural of Siddur) have been written to account for the widely varying and finely shaded interpretations of the Jewish religion around the world.

Two of the most important prayers in Judaism are the Amidah, which consists of 19 benedictions or blessings and is incorporated into all three weekday prayers and all four Sabbath prayers, and the Shema Yisrael, which is the centerpiece of all morning and evening prayers. The Kaddish, a collection of entreaties and blessings, is another important prayer. It's usually chanted. Lastly is the Aleinu, a brief set of words usually said at the end of each prayer session.

Jewish prayers are read aloud and while doing so the reader/prayee is supposed to concentrate on what he or she is saying. In the case of the Amidah, the temple congregation usually repeats each blessing after the Rabbi. One other odd requirement is that a quorum of ten other practicing Jews must be present during the prayer, unless that's just not possible, in which case you can go ahead solo. Following is a general but orthodox guide for the weekday morning, afternoon and evening prayers, called in order Shacharit, Mincha, and Ma'ariv. If you're doing this for the first time, clear your daily calendar. You're going to be reading more text than an English grad student in May.

You Will Need

A quorum

Fringed prayer shawl known as a tallit

A copy of the Siddur

Copies of the Bible and the Torah

Steps to Enlightenment

1 ◌ Right when you wake up, put on the tallit.

2 ◌ Next read aloud the first part of the Shema Yisrael.

3 ◌ Once that's done, read aloud Psalms 100 and 145–150 as well as Exodus chapters 14 and 15 both of which are known in Jewish circles as the Song at the Sea.

4 ◌ Now it's time to read the rest of the Shema Yisrael.

5 ◌ Doing all nineteen blessings in the Amidah is the final step to the Shacharit or morning prayers.

6 ◌ Afternoon prayers, or the Mincha, start with a reading of Psalm 84 chapter 28, verses 1 through 8, and from the Torah.

7 ◌ Next read aloud Malachi, chapter 3, verse 4.

8 ◌ Following Malachi, read Psalms 144m, 115, 141, and 145.

9 ◌ Then break out the Amidah again and go through all nineteen blessings.

10 ◌ Top off the morning prayers by chanting out the Kaddish.

11 ◌ Evening prayers, or Ma'ariv, start with the Shema Yisrael followed by the Hashkiveinu, which says "Lay us down to sleep, Adonai, our God, in peace, raise us erect, our King, to life, and spread over us the shelter of Your peace."

12 ◌ After that, recite the Kaddish and end with the Amidah.

Alternative and Lesser-Known Religions

As a growing number of people look for alternative ways to improve their spirituality and find enlightenment, there has been an intense revival of interest in some of the world's oldest religions as well as a concerted effort by the world's most inspired (and sometimes totally wacko) individuals to create new ways of nurturing the soul. Even though you'll find your fair share of UFO cults and guru-driven followings, there are several ideas worth taking a look at.

Neo-Pagan Religions

Neo-pagan religions are updated forms of the oft-misrepresented and persecuted Pagan religions. The term Pagan was given to ancient religions by Christians and it simply refers to groups who based their ceremonies, symbols, and gods on cultures that existed before the Christian religion. Ancient Egyptian, Greek, and Celtic cultures played large roles in these Pagan followings (and to a certain extent still do). Neo-pagan religions focus on the earth and the cycles of nature as a source for spirituality. Wicca and Druidism are two of the more popular groups to have revived themselves in the past twenty years or so, although there are at least a dozen others including the Fellowship of Isis and Shamanism.

Wicca

Wicca is the modern form of the religion known as witchcraft and it has one of the fastest growing followings in North America. And no, these folks don't go around dressed up in black pointy hats and they are not the spawn of Satan. Nor is the practice solely for women. There are lots of men Wiccans too and contrary to the many fine reruns of *Bewitched* they are not called warlocks.

The Wicca religion, which is sometimes referred to as The Craft, is based on ancient Celtic cultures and symbols. Over the years these beliefs were modified with ceremonies and forms of magic that include fertility rituals (for both plants, animals, and humans) and medicinal cures. These days, Wiccans worship nature and the pleasures of life as the path to enlightenment, rather than a spiritual afterlife. And yes, they do perform spells.

It's quite easy to find books on the subject (including *The Complete Idiot's Guide to Wicca and Witchcraft*). Several of the most revered are also still in print, including *The God of the Witches* (1931) by Margaret Murray and *Witchcraft Today* (1954) by Gerald Gardener.

Wiccan Lovers Spell

Wiccan prayer comes in the form of spells and magic charms, but the Wiccan moral code or Rede—which is essentially "do whatever you want as long as it doesn't manipulate or hurt anyone including yourself"—means that the idea of evil spells and the whole good witch-bad witch theory is just a product of the Inquisition and bad '70s television. Essentially, a spell consists of a few candles lit, some phrases said, and some intense concentration—a combination found in most of the mainstream religions. This love spell isn't meant to make someone fall in love with you. It's to reinforce an already loving relationship. Oh, and it works only on or just before a full moon, of course.

You Will Need:

One bottle of red wine or grape juice
Sprig of fresh rosemary
Two cinnamon sticks
One vanilla pod
A photo of your lover

Steps to Enlightenment

1 ✿ Mix the rosemary, cinnamon, and vanilla together in a bowl.

2 ✿ Study the photo of your sweetheart and recall the intimate details of that day together, including the emotions you felt at the time.

3 ✿ Then put the herbs and spices inside a bottle of red wine or grape juice and as you are doing this say the following words:

> *Entwined as one we shall be,*
> *Pure love forever,*
> *Just you and me.*
> *From this chalice we drink this wine,*
> *Imbued with passion,*
> *Till the end of time.*

4 ✿ That night, drink the wine with your lover.

Druidry

Contrary to what you might think, Druids are not short hairy men that like to prance naked at Stonehenge. They can be any type of person while dancing naked around Stonehenge. Like Wicca, Druidry or Druidism dates back to

Celtic cultures and perhaps even before then. And indeed, there is speculation that Druids built Stonehenge in England as a place of worship, which is why groups of Druids still converge on the monument during the yearly solstices. Though they categorize Druidism as a religion, many Druids think of it as a philosophy that can be followed in tandem with another major religion.

Druidism is a practice that has a high level of love and respect for nature and the natural world—especially oak and other trees. In fact the word Druid comes from the Greek word *drus*, meaning oak, and the Indo-European word *wid*, meaning knowledge or wisdom. Druid therefore means "having knowledge of the oak." In essence, Druids believe that life is for learning and gaining knowledge through on-going experience, whether that's through reading books, hiking in the Alps, or dancing at a full moon party in Thailand. That said, Druids believe that in life they are to follow the Celtic virtues of honor, loyalty, hospitality, honesty, justice, and courage as they pursue their own individual paths to enlightenment.

Books on the subject are easy to find and include Ross Nichols's *Book of Druidry* (1990) and *The Druids: Celtic Priests of Nature* (1999) by Jean Markale. If you're looking to join up with a group, two of the most popular are the Ancient Druid Order and the Order of Bards, Ovates and Druids, both in the United Kingdom. In the United States, there's the Henge of Keltria and the Reformed Druids of North America.

Ancient Chinese Religions

Though Buddhism made a big mark on Chinese cultures, its other two "official" religions over the centuries were Taoism and Confucianism, both more life philosophies than God-worshiping religions.

Taoism

Taoism (pronounced Dow-ism) is part life philosophy and part religion and was created in China in the sixth century BCE by a man named Lao-tzu, who was eager to figure out a way to live peacefully and mean-ingfully while war after war raged in his homeland. What he came up with was the Tao or the Way. In essence, the Tao refers to the force that flows through all life. Its teachings set out some suggestions on how to live life as a part of the flow. Scholars of Taoism say that the Tao cannot be defined but only learned through experience. So if you're interested, get out there and start practicing.

Taoists believe that everything in the natural world flows in a physical and spiritual life force. By recognizing this flow, Taoists believe they can fend off chaos, gain hope, and become one with the ordered and enlightened universe. Recognizing the flow or the Way can be done by developing and demonstrating certain virtues known as the Three Jewels: compassion, moderation, and humility. Also, Taoists believe in *wu wei*, an idea embodying the concept that nature should be allowed to take its course without any manmade interruption. By getting in the way of nature, one would only unbalance the harmony or the opposites inherent in the universe (represented by the yin and yang symbol). However, if the life force or energy is unbalanced, a Taoist can seek to correct the flow through practices such as acupuncture, meditation, and martial arts.

The *Tao Te Ching* is an instructional and philosophical set of lyrical poems written by Lao-tzu and is still widely read by Taoists for inspiration and for tips on how to best follow the Way.

Confucianism

Confucianism got its start in the sixth century BCE in China by a man known as Confucius, who went on to corner the fortune-cookie market. Before then, however, he taught a set of ethics that combined the Taoist beliefs about nature with the Buddhist beliefs of reincarnation and achieving total enlightenment. These ethics were meant to give individuals a moral set of goals by which to live. There are still about six million followers of Confucius in China.

Essentially, those who practice Confucianism try to live their lives with a sense of ritual and love for family while being righteous, honest, trustworthy, benevolent to those in need, and loyal to the state.

A good book on Confucius's life and teachings is *Confucius: The Golden Rule* by Russell Freedman and Frederic Clement.

Esoteric Followings

In *Webster's New College Dictionary,* the word esoteric is defined as: "Intended for or understood only by a particular group." Which makes sense when referring to these types of spiritual followings. They are very secretive because they believe that they are guarding ancient and secret knowledge that's been passed down to them for thousands of years. Members achieve total enlightenment through reading and by being taught a complex series of physical exercises and instructions— sometimes mystical—on how to live life.

Gurdjieff's Teachings

Named for George Ivanovitch Gurdjieff (1866–1949), a modern day guru who grew up in the Near East and learned ancient wisdom, yoga, and mysticism from Tibet and Central Asia, this following is a combination of mystic Christianity, psychology, numerology, and sacred neo-pagan dancing. It is steeped in secretive practices and is only open to those who are members. To become a member, one has to be deemed "ready" for the teaching and invited into the group by a present member to meet with the teacher, a highly revered person often referred to as the Man Who Knows. Modern groups who practice the Gurdjieff philosophy are sometimes called the Fourth Way School and they are hard to find, though definitely present in New York City and possibly in other major cities in the United States and Europe.

There's a lot to this following, but basically Gurdjieff taught that most of us never truly know our true selves or our "I" because of the roles we were brought up with and because of the perpetual state of unthinking habit we live in. In other words, we are sleepwalking through life, which prevents us from becoming our true selves and blocks our way to spiritual enlightenment. Gurdjieff taught his students that in order to wake up and live their lives to their fullest, they had to submit themselves to the will of a teacher while doing a series of difficult physical workouts, breathing exercises, and sacred dances.

A book that is considered required reading by some Gurdjieff-inspired esoteric groups is *In Search of the Miraculous: Fragments of an Unknown Teaching* by P. D. Ouspensky. Ouspensky was one of Gurdjieff's students in the '20s before the guru died.

Self-Help or Personal Development Groups

These groups aren't secret at all. In fact, there are so many books written on the effective techniques of successful people or on finding ways to be more confident, organized, loving, forgiving, and, yes, enlightened that some people probably wish they were more secret. Regardless, for the past seventy-five years or so, the business of self-help has taken off both in book form and in group get-togethers. They are not religious in nature, though some verge into the spiritual. Instead, these groups teach individuals how to be more successful at everything they do, whether that's working in an office, being in a relationship, or searching for total enlightenment. The following two groups have had their share of controversy over the years because of their odd ball methodology. I recommend taking a good long objective look before joining up.

Scientology

The Church of Scientology was set up by L. Ron Hubbard, science fiction author turned guru whose book *Dianetics*—which was written in 1950—is the basis for the group's belief system. With a little psychological therapy, some good old-fashioned confession, a dash of religious myth, and a big portion of science fiction thrown into the mix, Scientology claims that one can achieve enlightenment by clearing the mind of past, suppressed memories of harmful or emotionally painful events known as engrams. These engrams, which can be compared to mental images buried in our subconscious, are removed when a person combs through his or her past in the presence of an approved "auditor" who helps the patient, er, member along by asking pertinent questions. When a bad memory or engram comes up in conversation, the auditor identifies it and then it is removed with the help of a small electrode machine similar to the machine used for lie detector tests. And you thought Hinduism was way out in left field . . .

Once all a person's engrams have been removed over a period of many months, then that person is declared "Clear." He or she is then able to be his or her true self, free of fear and anxiety. There are many more facets to this philosophy/religion, including the fact that we not only have engrams from this life, but from a series of past lives as well. There's also some really far-out stuff that you can do after you're "Cleared."

If you want to read more, the main book laying out Scientology is, of course, *Dianetics*. There have been a number of other books as well as newspaper and magazine articles written about the church in recent years because of ongoing controversies within the group and because of revelations (not always positive) about the group's practices by ex-members. After going into total seclusion in 1980, after which only a handful of people ever saw him again, Hubbard officially died in 1986 (though unofficially some believe he passed away as early as 1983).

Landmark Forum

The Landmark Education group is another self-help group that has a growing following, at least among those who can afford the $400 three-day start-up Landmark Forum course. It does not offer religion but rather seminars that they claim can help people positively change the way they live through improved communication, heightened self-esteem, and better relationships. Similar to Gurdjieff's philosophy, the Landmark Forum teaches that we must break out of our traditional habits in order to see and act differently so that we may improve our lives. Some who have taken the course claim that it has improved their married lives or their relationships with their children while allowing them to excel professionally. Others claim that it is a manipulative cultlike process that can cause emotional breakdowns while brain-washing its students into emptying their bank accounts.

The roots of Landmark Education are based in the est training of the 1970s that was started by a former used-car and encyclopedia salesman named Werner Erhard (est stands for Erhard Seminars Training). Erhard is said to have been influenced by some time spent in the Church of Scientology and by studying Alan Watts–style Modern Buddhism. In 1991, some former est employees started up Landmark Education and Erhard subsequently sold them the rights to his teachings after *60 Minutes* did a scathing exposé on the shady methods est used with its followers.

The way it works is that you pay the admission fee and then spend an entire weekend (from morning to midnight) in a giant conference room with as many as 150 other people. The meetings are rigorous and the breaks are few and far between. Some have compared these seminars to boot camp. They are highly controlled and teachers seek to break students down emotionally and then build them back up. Apparently, the seminars can become quite emotional and they are described as alternately inspiring and exhausting. Some are really turned off at the end of the weekend when another teacher walks in the room and gives you a hard sell about coming to (and paying for) the next series of seminars. In fact, a good portion of these seminars is spent urging (some say manipulating) you to bring others to the program with the inference being that your time spent at the Forum won't be a total success unless you bring in others to the next seminar.

Those interested can log on to the Landmark Web site at www. landmarkeducation.com. There have been some newspaper and magazine articles written about taking the Landmark Forum. One to check out was published in *New York Magazine* in July 2001. It's entitled *Welcome to EST: The Next Generation*.

How to Know If You're the Chosen One

If you get the feeling you're the Chosen One, it may be helpful to check first with a therapist. Lots of folks who think they're "the next big thing" or "God's gift to humankind" are really just annoying egomaniacs. Others could just have a God complex from growing up with parents who told them they could be anything they wanted when the hard reality is that you have to be smart and work hard to get what you want. Still others might be in the beginning stages of mental illness, and if you don't get a hold of all this Chosen One nonsense, you're going to end up in a nice padded room writing on the walls with your toes. That said, if this isn't the first time you've had the feeling of being the Chosen One and it has become a rather persistent gnawing reality, then there are some things you can check to make sure before asking about prescriptions.

You Will Need:

A mirror (to check your scalp)
A comfort and knowledge of your deepest emotions
An open heart
Self-confidence
Knowledge of everything

Steps to Enlightenment

1 ✪ Check your head. At the first thought that you might be the Chosen One, check your scalp for any strange marks or tattoos. If you see the number 6 etched onto your head three times, this is the mark of the devil and you are not the Chosen One but the Antichrist, a big thing to consider in its own right but out of the scope of this particular set of instructions.

2 ✪ Check yourself. Take special notice of your feelings. Do you feel enlightened? If not, then you may not be the Chosen One. Try eating a giant chocolate bar or traveling in the Himalayas for a few months and then check back in on this step when you're done.

3 ✪ Test the waters. By this I don't mean go out and try to walk on water, especially if you can't swim. There are less elaborate ways to check your Chosen status. If you do feel enlightened and there is no strange tattoo on your scalp (if you paid someone to put it there one drunk night it doesn't count as divine), try loving every living thing. If you can sincerely feel and give love for a guy selling double- and triple-A batteries on the New York subway or for all politicians regardless of party affiliation, then you may truly be the Chosen One.

4 ✪ Test some more. Go out into the streets and try to save someone's soul. Touching them lightly on the head may work. If not, explain that you saw a bug and you were trying to get it off. Another tack may be to get a soapbox and a megaphone and try preaching to passersby. Take note of whether or not anyone cares or if they just look at you and hold their purses a little closer.

5 ✪ The final test of whether or not you are the Chosen One is your ability to be all-knowing. If you're having trouble figuring out what the capital of South Dakota is, then forget it.

Word to the Wise

If you've gone through the steps over and over and after three years you still can't figure out whether or not you are truly the Chosen One, this might be cause for concern. Signs that might require checks in the "No" column are that you have become wildly bearded, have started putting rocks in your shoes, or have been arguing a lot lately with your loved ones about why they keep calling the men in white with the straitjackets. If all these are true, then sorry Charlie. Take the pills and do something else.

How to Have a Backyard Tent Revival

The blind see! A lady walks from her wheelchair! Healing, Miracles, Salvation! Seeing these words pasted up around town was a sure sign there was going to be a good old-fashioned southern tent revival in the neighborhood. They were always held in the summer, usually for a week, when the heat could remind sinners of hell and the promise of enlightenment was as certain as the sweaty preacher's voice was loud. Going to one of these was like going to a carnival sideshow and barbecue, except instead of pecan pie, you got Jesus for dessert.

But why wait for a revival to set up in your neighborhood when you can throw a one-day event yourself right in your backyard. At the very least, it's a great way to get your friends together for some good music and entertainment. That's good for your soul regardless of whether anyone actually gets talked into finding Jesus.

You Will Need:

An open-air tent with no sides
A small stage for the preacher and band to set up on
A preacher
A band
Folding chairs
Nearby body of water or, lacking that, a large outdoor tub
     (for baptizing)
A basket or tray (to collect donations)
Signs to advertise for the event around the neighborhood
A crowd of sinners and believers

Steps to Enlightenment

1 ✷ The first goal of any tent revivalist is to get people interested in their big party. Do this by passing out fliers adorned with big bold red letters that read "One Powerful Night Under the Big Top," "See the Lame Walk," "Come Get Saved!" and that sort of thing.

2 ✷ Next you'll want to hire a band. A gospel band would be the obvious choice but jazz bands or acoustic guitarists work nicely, as do rock outfits as long as they're not singing about the devil.

3 ✷ If you can hire a preacher, more power to you. Doing this yourself, however, will really add to the zest of the afternoon. As in traditional tent revivals, the important thing is to preach with much fire-and-brimstone drama and theatrics. Make sure to stomp from one side of the stage to the other and do much hand and arm waving. Weep over the crucifixion, rant about visions of hell, act tormented over examples of sinning and sinful lives (including your own) and how those in the audience can receive salvation if only they give their lives over to Jesus.

4 ✷ Get some friends to cooperate with you on this and occasionally yell out things like "Can I have an amen?!" to which they'll reply

"Amen!" Get them to periodically yell out "Preach it brother!" to add to the zeal of the moment. The goal is to work the crowd up into a religious frenzy so that a) they can feel the power of the spirit and b) they'll put some change in the donation basket to help offset the cost of renting the tent.

5 ✿ On that note, be sure to pass around the donation basket at the end of the first hour. After that you can ask for money as often as you like throughout the day. One common tent revival practice is to put the basket on the stage and after the preaching is done and the congregation is in a fine frenzy, get them to come up to the stage and give. At this point it doesn't hurt to tell everyone who they can make checks out to. It's also a good time to announce the sale of any T-shirts, stickers, or CDs that the band might have recorded.

6 ✿ As the revival is coming to a close, it's important to ask people in the audience to come to the front to accept Jesus. When they do this, place your hands on their heads to invest the Lord into them (either that or give them a strong thumbs-up).

7 ✿ Baptize these new converts in a nearby river or lake by gently dunking them under the water. More fun is to have a large tub nearby so that everyone can witness the baptizing right on the spot.

Building Shrines

Household shrines have long been a part of the spiritual path, especially for Buddhists, Hindus, and Elvis fans. It is believed that by having images of the object of your faith (or adoration, as is the case when it comes to enshrining the King of Rock and Roll), you are inviting that person or God into your home on a daily basis to sit with them, give them thanks, and ask for enlightened guidance.

Hindu Shrine

Hindus believe that the statues or images of their gods on shrines in their homes offer real-life, though temporary, bodies for their gods to channel into the home and bless them on a daily basis. Really, there is no end to how many gods or goddesses you can include on a Hindu shrine but most practicing Indians choose either Shiva or Vishnu as the central figure, with various incarnations, wives, and attendants surrounding them. It's also common to include a god that can help you with something you feel is missing in your life such as Lakshmi, the goddess of wealth, or Kama, the god of love.

You Will Need:

An area of the house to reserve for the shrine
Images or statues of the gods of your choice
Bowls for daily *puja* or offering
Candles
Incense
Flowers
Food
Water
Copy of Hindu scripture such as the Bhagavad Gita or the Upanishads

Steps to Enlightenment

1 ☙ Place a table or set of shelves in an area of the house where it won't be disturbed. This area should also be big enough to allow you or your entire family to sit while doing the daily *puja* or offerings. Some Hindu families have entire rooms devoted to a shrine, but this isn't necessary. The shrine should be near to the floor, but not on it, to make the *puja* easier to perform (you'll sit on the floor for this).

2 ☙ Place the main god, such as Shiva or Vishnu, in the center of the shrine and the images of lesser gods around it. It's also common to

place images of your father and mother here as well as an image of your guru or the family's guru to show respect.

3 ✿ There is no order in which the various bowls and offerings need to be placed on the shrine. Just make sure that they are below the images of the gods or goddesses represented there.

Word to the Wise

Upkeep of a Hindu shrine is very important. Gods don't like channeling into messy rooms, where the shrines have old, decaying food and dirty water. Be sure to replenish the offerings daily (a practicing Hindu would be performing *puja* daily and replenishing the food and flowers then anyway). Also, if a statue or image gets broken, ripped, or damaged in any way, you'll have to replace it.

Shrine to Buddha

Buddhist shrines may be physical pedestals, but they aren't metaphorical pedestals on which to place the Buddha. After all, Siddhartha Gautama was just a man, albeit a very important one who achieved Total Enlightenment and transcended the endless cycle of life, death, and rebirth. Still, a statue of Buddha in the home on a shrine is a way to remind you of his teachings while offering respect. It's also a way to spend some peaceful time in his company.

The most important thing to keep in mind when setting up your shrine to Buddha is that the objects you place on it should all help to remind you of the Buddha's enlightened qualities, which you are trying to emulate in order to help others to achieve enlightenment. Every shrine should have a representative of the Buddha's body, which can be in the form of a statue or an image; his speech, which should be some kind of Buddhist scripture such as the text of the Four Noble Truths; and his enlightened mind, which is usually represented by a miniature stupa, a pointed dome that is the structure for most Buddhist temples.

You Will Need:

A table or shelf, preferably with multiple levels

A peaceful place in the house

Statue or image of Buddha

Text of the Four Noble Truths

A small stupa made out of any material

Eight bowls containing the following:

> Drinking water
>
> Water for washing hands and feet
>
> A flower
>
> Incense
>
> A small candle
>
> Scented water
>
> A small portion of food
>
> A seashell or a small bell

Steps to Enlightenment

1 ✪ A table or shelf can work fine for a Buddhist shrine or it's possible to build one yourself. In either case make sure the statue or image of the Buddha will be higher than the level of your head when you are sitting down. Also, the shrine should be in a peaceful, uncluttered, and clean place. It should face east because Siddhartha Gautama was facing east when he achieved total enlightenment under the bodhi tree. If possible, have a structure with more than one level so that the offerings will all be placed below the level of the Buddha. If this isn't possible, one simple solution might be to place the Buddha on a block or small shelf on top of the shrine.

2 ✪ Place the statue or image of the Buddha in the center of the shrine.

3 ✷ Some Buddhist text or scripture should be placed to the left of the Buddha (on his right).

4 ✷ The stupa goes to the Buddha's right (on his left).

5 ✷ Place all eight bowls in a straight line in front of the Buddha. If you have a lower level to your shrine, they should go there. According to ancient instructions, the distance between each bowl should be about the width of a grain of wheat. If you don't happen to have any wheat around, then three centimeters apart will do fine.

6 ✷ The offerings inside the bowls should be, in order from right to left: drinking water, washing water, flower, incense, candle, scented water, and seashell or bell. These offerings represent all the senses: sight, smell, taste, touch, and hearing (the seashell is the sound of liberation).

Word to the Wise

It's important to replenish the offerings each day while putting the food and flowers outside where birds and animals can eat them. This helps develop generosity and lessen stinginess, while accumulating lots of good karma.

Shrine to Elvis

The King of Rock and Roll is probably more enshrined in the United States than Buddha or any Hindu God, and with good reason. Not only did Elvis break down the doors of popular music with a twangy guitar and a snarl, but he gyrated and twisted his hips enough onstage to enlighten an entire generation of young girls. These days there's all kinds of cool Elvis paraphernalia you can include in a shrine, including an Elvis toilet, Elvis stamps, and Elvis lunchboxes. For this shrine, the more the merrier.

You Will Need:

A table

An image of Elvis, preferably of the painted black velvet kind

Lots and lots of Elvis stuff

Candles

A recording of Elvis's "Love Me Tender"

Steps to Enlightenment

1 ✿ Home-based Elvis shrines can be anywhere inside or outside the house, from the living room to the backyard to the bedroom, which is the location of choice for many aging female Elvis fans who believe that images and statues of the rock and roller will channel the King right into their beds where they will be able to express their undying love for him.

2 ✿ In general, it is recommended that your shrine be in as public a place as possible so that all who enter will know of your devotion. Next to the stereo system is a good spot, as you'll want to play Elvis hits while you gaze upon his image.

3 ✿ If possible, place your shrine so that it faces a bathroom. This is a way to recognize and commemorate how the King achieved a relieving enlightenment before meeting his ignominious but wholly satisfying end.

4 ✿ A central image of the King is the preeminent concern and these can come in many forms, from posters to Warhol prints. Vintage black velvet paintings lit with a small black light beneath the image have particular merit.

5 ✿ Offerings to Elvis come in many forms and the rule on what to include on the shrine is that there are no rules. Most of the stuff should

have an image of the King on it, but it's fine to prop up snapshots of you in front of Graceland or alongside any particularly wacky public Elvis shrines around the world.

6 ☯ As with any shrine, candles will round out the magical contemplative feel and look you're going for. You'll also be able to light one each year to mourn the King's passing (August 16, 1977).

Word to the Wise

Shrines to Elvis have a tendency to grow at a rapid pace, due to the immense number of kitschy crafts and Elvis-related gifts in the world. There is a danger of having these shrines take over entire houses and they can sometimes give the shrine builder an Elvis complex, in which he or she actually takes on the appearance of the King. Indeed, if you find yourself dressed in white bell-bottom jumpsuits while wearing pasted-on sideburns and large silver sunglasses, put down the Elvis ashtray and step away from the Elvis puzzle. It might be time to get enlightenment elsewhere.

Sail forth—steer for the deep waters only,
Reckless O soul, exploring, I with thee, and thou with me,
For we are bound where mariner has not yet dared to go.
And we will risk the ship, ourselves and all.

—WALT WHITMAN

c h a p t e r
TWO

The Spiritual Triad: Mind, Body, and Soul

During the pursuit of total enlightenment it's important to stay balanced. Too much time spent in church or at temple makes Jack a dull boy. Secluding yourself with books or working ten hours a day means there'll be no outdoor fun. Plus, you'll lessen your chances of meeting someone and falling in love. In other words, you need a healthy body, a sharp mind, and spiritual fulfillment in order to find total enlightenment.

Part I: Mind

It is not enough to have a good mind: one must use it well.

—Descartes

It has been said that sharpening the mind is the way to enlightenment, but that's only because once you know how to do something you can physically go out and practice it. Still, those who neglect the mind,

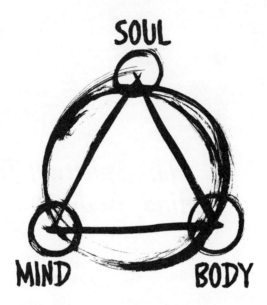

either by not expanding it or by not removing the emotional clutter it collects, are missing out on some really exciting enlightenment.

Books for Enlightenment: A List

There's no better way to inform the mind than reading. In addition to the very book you hold in your hands, many of the following will also inform the soul.

1 ✿ *The Snow Leopard,* by Peter Matthiessen

2 ✿ *Pablo Neruda: Selected Poems,* Nathaniel Tarn, editor

3 ✿ *Siddhartha,* by Herman Hesse

4 ✿ *Gravity's Rainbow,* by Thomas Pynchon

5 ✷ *The Hero with a Thousand Faces,* by Joseph Campbell

6 ✷ *The Complete Shorter Poems,* by Kenneth Rexroth

7 ✷ *The Teachings of Don Juan,* by Carlos Casteñeda

8 ✷ *The Sacred Path of the Warrior,* by Chogyam Trungpa

9 ✷ *Zen and the Art of Motorcycle Maintenance,* by Robert Pirsig

10 ✷ *Memories, Dreams, Reflections,* by Carl Jung

Clear the Mind:
Simple Meditation Techniques

*"The soul that moves in the world of the senses and yet keeps
the senses in harmony . . . finds rest in quietness."*

—Bhagavad Gita

Rooted in the Buddhist and Hindu religions, the practice of meditation has been around for centuries. Because of this, hundreds of techniques have come about, with some people suggesting that prayer in any form and from any religion is a type of meditation in itself. No matter how you meditate, your basic goal is to quiet the mind of its normal busy and distracted state while focusing on the present moment. In this way, you can free yourself of worry, depression, and stress, which if left unchecked, can affect the body in the form of tense muscles, headaches, and low energy. Not only is this painful, but it's a certainty that you won't get enlightenment if it goes on for long.

The classic form of meditation is to find a quiet place, sit crosslegged or in the "lotus" pose, with hands on your knees, back straight, and eyes closed. It is still the most effective method.

You Will Need:

A quiet place
Comfortable loose clothes (although anything will do)
You and your soon-to-be-clear mind

Steps to Enlightenment

1 ✿ Find a quiet spot in the house and if need be lay down a blanket or something soft.

2 ✿ Unplug phones and generally make sure you won't be disturbed for at least fifteen minutes.

3 ✿ Sit on the floor and face in the direction you feel most comfortable, preferably not facing a wall or any other obstacle (many people sit facing east, toward the rising sun). Make sure your legs are crossed with your back straight and chest slightly out. You won't find "hunching over" in any yoga guide.

4 ✿ Now breathe in deeply through your nose, using your diaphragm in your abdomen to fill up your lungs. Then exhale slowly out of your mouth, completely emptying your lungs.

5 ✿ Close your eyes and start to focus on inhaling and exhaling slowly and steadily.

6 ✿ As distractions or thoughts enter your mind, just never mind them. Simply exhale them away with your breathing.

7 ✿ Think of nothing. Focus your attention on the gentle rise and fall of your abdomen and the slow rhythm of your breathing.

8 ✺ After several minutes your breathing should get slower and deeper as you begin to relax.

9 ✺ Continue this procedure for about fifteen minutes, once or twice a day.

Word to the Wise

When you first start meditation you will be surprised at how difficult it is to not pay attention to your thoughts. They will be like a ringing telephone that you want to answer for fear that you're missing an important call. This only means you need to meditate more than you thought you did. Simply let the thoughts come and then watch them go with your breath.

The Creative Process

Some say that art in any form is an expression of the soul. So it stands to reason that being creative—whether that's painting, writing, or photographing—is one way to find the soul. Luckily, everyone's brain has the capacity for logic (the left side) and creativity (the right side), so it shouldn't be too hard to cultivate an artistic path to enlightenment.

Writing Poetry: Basic Techniques

"And it was at that age. . . . Poetry arrived
in search of me. . . .
. . . And I, infinitesimal being,
drunk with the great starry
void,
likeness, image of

> *mystery,*
> *felt myself a pure part*
> *of the abyss,*
> *I wheeled with the stars,*
> *my heart broke loose on the wind."*

—Pablo Neruda, *Poetry*

Poetry has been the outlet for star-crossed lovers and inspired spiritualists for as long as man has known how to write. A poem can be a sculpture of words on paper and a song when read out loud. In fact, there's no better way to express your enlightenment than with a poem, even if you're the only one who ever reads it (which may be the case more often than not). For those who find themselves weak-in-the-knees in love, hunt down your favorite pen, then loosen up your writing hand. It's all the inspiration you'll need.

You Will Need:

Paper
A pen
To be in love

Steps to Enlightenment

1 ❂ Try not to stare too much at a blank sheet of paper. That will only make you feel pressured to perform, which never works in any situation when in love. If you haven't already thought of a first line, just go ahead and start writing about how you're feeling. Don't worry about rhyming or meter or breaking the words up into lines of any kind. This brainstorming is a great way to get loosened up and get used to seeing how emotions can be translated into words.

2 ✪ After about ten minutes of writing, go back and see if any words or phrases jump out at you.

3 ✪ Write down those words and phrases in separate lines. Again, don't worry about meter or rhyme just yet.

4 ✪ Once you have a fair amount of lines to work with, meter them into iambic pentameter with the following pattern: da-DUM/da-DUM/da-DUM/da-DUM/da-DUM. Basically, this means that a hard emphasis should come on each second syllable (called a "foot" in academic circles). To write iambic pentameter, you'll need five feet per line. Example: How do I love thee—Let me count the ways (how DO/I LOVE/thee LET/me COUNT/the WAYS).

5 ✪ As for rhyme, you could choose to write a sonnet, which is perfect for love poems. The most popular kind of sonnet is the Shakespearean sonnet, made famous by the bard himself. These are fourteen lines long, broken down into four rhyming parts. Here's the scheme: a-b-a-b/c-d-c-d/e-f-e-f/g-g. Each letter represents a line that should rhyme with its corresponding letter. The structure is officially known as three quatrains and a couplet.

Word to the Wise

Most poets these days have nothing to do with meter and rhyme, preferring to stick to their own kind of free verse. If you go this route—and you definitely should at least try it, especially if this is an exercise in self-expression, which it is—be sure and read your poem out loud to yourself and tweak the words so that you have some kind of rhythm going. Pablo Neruda once said that if a poem doesn't sing, it's not finished.

Painting: Basic Techniques

When you find yourself at a loss for words, colors and shapes can take their place. Plus, you don't have to be the next van Gogh to find enlightenment with a paintbrush. All it takes is a few supplies and a willingness to get paint on your hands.

You Will Need:

Acrylic paints with primary colors (titanium white, Mars black, phthalo green, cadmium orange, cadmium red medium, cadmium yellow medium, phthalo blue, yellow ochre, and dioxide purple. Burnt sienna, burnt umber, and raw titanium are useful if you're painting skin tones.)

A pencil and pencil sharpener

A variety of brushes (start with a medium-size round pointed, a medium flat, and a larger flat)

Canvases, canvas boards, or paper

An easel or something to lean your canvas on

A palette to put paint on (cardboard will work okay)

A bowl of water

Paper towels

A subject (i.e., something to paint)

Extremely optional and not recommended in any way: a knife to remove your ear out of tortured inspiration

Steps to Enlightenment

1 ✿ For still-life painting, gather a few objects from around your house and set them up in an inspirational place (failing that, the kitchen table will do fine). If you're painting people or houses, find a photo and tape

it to a rigid piece of cardboard. Taking your easel outdoors and setting up in front of a scene (urban, country, or otherwise) is also good.

2 ✿ Using a pencil, very lightly sketch the boundaries of your subject on the canvas. Abstract expressionists can skip the pencil altogether and go straight to the paint.

3 ✿ Squeeze out several colors on your palette. Then spray or shake some water over them to keep them moist while you work.

4 ✿ Look closely at your subject for any subtle colors that might be showing themselves. As one teacher recommends, "Don't just look for the blue in a cloud." If you're color blind, stick to meditation.

5 ✿ Start painting. If you're having trouble starting, do some practice strokes on a piece of scrap paper. And remember—if you feel like you've messed up, you can always paint over your mistakes.

6 ✿ When you're done for the day, rinse out all brushes thoroughly with clean water. Acrylic paint, when dried, will turn to plastic and so will your brushes if they're not rinsed.

Word to the Wise

Don't worry about making "mistakes" or not getting the color right. If you're just starting out, your style will slowly show itself, so just relax and enjoy the process of painting. As Henry Miller said, "Somewhere along the way one discovers that what one has to tell is not nearly so important as the telling itself."

Mind-Altering Drugs

People throughout the ages have talked about and reported on visions of seeing God or communicating with spirits. Maybe these were divinely influenced. Maybe the folks talking about visions found some high-grade psychedelic mushrooms. Drugs have played a role in many spiritual quests from early Native American shamans to rave dancing in Goa, India. For some, it is thought that by taking hallucinogenics, you actually enter the spirit world where you can communicate with your God, and then, as was the case with the Native American shamans, you can bring back and teach what you've learned to the people who didn't get to take the drugs.

Peyote

The small round peyote cactus is a highly intoxicating and hallucinogenic plant that has been used in Native American ceremonies for centuries. Made famous by Carlos Casteñeda's book *The Teachings of Don Juan,* in which the author gobbled up a few "buttons" and wandered the deserts of the southwest with an aging shaman, peyote was used to influence or contact the spirit world. The plant itself was thought to be a messenger that allows someone to talk to God without the services of a priest—a sort of do-it-yourself, all-in-one church experience.

These days, members of the Native American Church still use peyote as a general healing tonic (it is believed to be a cure for alcoholism) and for a variety of ceremonies, including weddings. If you are a member of the church (one is the Peyote Way Church of God in Wilcox, Arizona), you can legally grow and harvest peyote for consumption in these ceremonies. Otherwise, it's a federal crime to have peyote in your possession. The main supply of peyote for Native Americans in the United States and Canada comes from several small growers in South Texas.

After the top part of the cactus is cut off (this is known as the button), it is ground up and either added to water to make tea or eaten dry. After ingesting peyote, your eyes will dilate and you will experience depression and fear while most likely becoming nauseous and vomiting. Getting sick during a peyote ceremony sounds like a total drag but it's important: It's thought that this is how the peyote cleanses your body and mind of impurities. Once this first phase is over, you will start to have feelings of euphoria and exhilaration and you will begin to hallucinate, or, say some, enter the spirit world.

Peyote is not a recreational drug, or at least it loses its spiritual power when taken as such. The ceremonies surrounding peyote are elaborate and help cultivate communication with the spirits. To host a ceremony, you'll need a guide with experience. The Native Americans call this guide a Road Man.

You Will Need:

Peyote buttons, crushed dry and made into tea

A remote location

A clear night (these last from midafternoon to sunup)

A tepee or similar structure with a fire pit in the middle

Cedar chips to throw on the fire

Several willing participants

Various musical instruments such as a drum, gourd rattle,
    and whistle

Steps to Enlightenment

1 ✿ When everyone has arrived at the ceremony at around 8 P.M., have each person sit in a circle around the fire pit. Then add some cedar chips to the fire to produce smoke, which symbolically cleanses the room.

2 ✺ Pass around the dry peyote and the peyote tea and instruct everyone to take one or the other, but not both.

3 ✺ After everyone has had some peyote, go around the circle and sing songs or tell stories.

4 ✺ After one hour, pass the peyote around again.

5 ✺ Repeat step 3.

6 ✺ Repeat step 4.

7 ✺ During this time, no one should leave the tent unless they must get sick. Afterward, it is very important that they come back in and join the circle.

8 ✺ At midnight, pass around water for everyone to drink. This is also a time for individuals to get up, leave the tepee, and take a break from the ceremony for about an hour. There may be some intoxicated prancing about, but that's normal.

9 ✺ After the break, songs and stories resume and prayers are spoken out loud as each individual feels moved to speak.

10 ✺ At dawn, a prayer to the morning sun is said. Then more water is passed around. And finally, a breakfast is served and eaten slowly.

Word to the Wise

Traditionally, only small amounts of peyote are taken at these ceremonies, so it doesn't take much to achieve total enlightenment. If you take too much, you might be enlightened for a whole week.

Marijuana and the Rastafarian Religion

Marijuana goes by many names (pot, weed, grass, and ganja, to name a few) and it has a long and troubled history in much of the world. Most people in this country associate the plant with either a good time or an evil influence, depending on who you talk to. But marijuana is known to have beneficial medicinal qualities and at least one group—the Rastafarians—officially use it as part of a spiritual ceremony.

One minor detail for Rastafarians and the Rastafarian religion, which originated in Jamaica and uses the Bible as its scripture, is that marijuana is illegal. Yes, even in Jamaica, if you're a Rasta you get no free pass with pot like the Native Americans and their peyote ceremonies do in the States. Instead, you get to spend some time in Jamaican jail, which is decidedly not enlightening, at least not in a good way.

As far as Rastafarians are concerned there is no clear reason why they can't smoke ganja legally. After all, they say, marijuana is advocated in the Bible: Psalms 104:14 says "He causeth the grass for the cattle, and *herb* for the service of man"; Exodus 10:12 says ". . . eat every *herb* of the land."

Critics, however, point out that the word "herb" could mean basil or St. Augustine or any of a hundred different things that are grown in the ground. Plus, there seems to be nowhere in the Bible where God, Jesus, or anyone else says ". . . and then roll it up and smoke it, mon." Call me crazy, but one has to wonder if all that pot smoking has blunted the Rastafarian interpretive skills. But then again, these are also the same people who worship as a deity Haile Selassie, former emperor of Ethiopia and a devout . . . Christian. Apparently, when a group of Rastafarians approached Selassie and told him he was the human form of their God, he asked them what the hell they were talking about and then told them to go away. But instead of getting discouraged, the Rastas were only strengthened by this spurn, saying the fact that Selassie denied he was God really meant that he was because God can't know himself. An odd logic, seeing as how God is thought to know quite a bit—some say everything. But there it is. It wouldn't be so far off base to call the Rastafarian religion the religion of self-delusion. In fact, that might be a better legal argument as to why they need to smoke so much "herb."

But we digress. The fact is, Rastafarians smoke marijuana because they believe it connects them with God. A ceremony known as the Binghi brings Rastas together to read and talk about the Bible and to smoke the herb, sing songs, dance, and play drums. More than anything, these get-togethers are about joy and fellowship, not about the smoke.

Part II: Body

When my creative energy flowed most freely,
my muscular activity was always greatest.

—Friedrich Nietzsche

The body, like the mind, can be a useful vehicle to help you along the path to enlightenment and that's really a matter of biology. Eating right and exercising more helps get the blood flowing and the endorphins active, which stimulates the mind, gets the core energy flowing, and relieves stress, giving you more time to contemplate your sweaty but totally hard navel. Yoga is perhaps the perfect mind-body-soul experience. And let's not forget sports or sport-like activities, where jumping out of an airplane or catching a thirty-five-foot wave are the modern-day equivalent of seeing God. With that kind of rush, who needs peyote?

Basic Health Tips

Being sick is a drag and no fun and definitely not the way to achieve total enlightenment. Avoid it at all costs with the help of the following five tips:

1 ✿ Eat right. Stuff in lots of whole grains, fruits, and vegetables and cut way back on the fat (yes, barbecued sausage and ribs, even those found in Lockhart, Texas, are loaded with lard). Also, avoid processed food like individually wrapped cheese slices. In fact, all cheese should be eaten seldomly, as should all dairy products, and then only the low-fat kind. Sounds boring but oh, the places you'll go!

2 ✿ Drink lots of fluids. Water is the elixir of life. Drink enough of it and your joints will no longer creak, you won't get as many common colds, and you'll be running to the toilet every fifteen minutes to let flow all those impurities that build up in your body. Urban myths everywhere say you should drink eight eight-ounce glasses a day.

3 ✪ Exercise. Aerobic exercise is the best, but just walking to the corner store instead of firing up the Caddy is good too. The idea is just to move your bones, get that heart pumping, the blood flowing, and the lungs expanding. The more new oxygen your body can get its mouth on, the better, and moving faster than normal is a good way to make that happen.

4 ✪ Drink wine. Yippee! Doctors now have evidence that one to three glasses of wine a day can lower cholesterol levels, prevent stomach ulcers, and even ward off cancer. Oh, and it's a good stress reliever too (after three glasses of wine, you could be so relieved of stress that you'll go right to bed). No wonder the French are so skinny and live long, unharried lives.

5 ✪ Laugh. I know it sounds funny, but giggling is good for your health. Experts say that when you have a good guffaw, you raise your blood pressure, but when you're done it goes down lower than it was before the joke (low blood pressure helps prevent heart disease). Also, when you laugh you take in lots more oxygen than when you don't laugh, thereby stimulating the brain. It's also good for the stomach muscles while helping you stay stress free. No joke!

Alternative Medicine

As Eastern medicine is becoming more accepted in the United States, more doctors are beginning to look at injuries and sicknesses as part of a bigger picture rather than an isolated situation. If you have continuous back problems, for example, one doctor who doesn't practice a holistic point of view might look at your spine and suggest traction or, in severe cases, surgery. A holistic doctor, on the other hand, would look at your back, but he or she would also look at how you sit and walk, how you sleep and work, and how you eat. The doctor would then recommend massage therapy or acupuncture to relieve pain. He or she may also suggest changes in chairs and desk positions or vitamin supplements and changes in diet to improve bone strength.

Among other things, this holistic approach to curing what ails you comes from the ancient practices of Chinese medicine. In China, doctors consider the body, like the natural world around it, as an ecosystem containing Five Elements: Fire, Earth, Metal, Water, and Wood. They also believe that good health is dependent on the balance of two opposing forces called Yin and Yang.

Chinese Medicine's Five Elements

The Five Elements, whose Chinese name is Wu Xing, are said to represent the basic cycles of nature (and therefore the human body). Taken separately, they are of no consequence, but together they feed off each other to perpetuate good health. Interestingly, the Chinese always link the elements with parts of the body and with corresponding emotions.

1 ✿ *Fire.* This first element represents light and energy and is embodied in the heart and small intestine. The emotion linked with Fire is joy, and too much joy in the form of overindulgence (with, let's say, an especially tasty Philly cheese steak sandwich with extra peppers) causes an imbalance. Those with an imbalance in fire energy may be a little down or depressed and have trouble sleeping. To gain fire, Chinese doctors recommend eating bitter dark vegetables such kale, beets, and collard greens.

2 ✪ *Earth.* The organs affected by the Earth element are the stomach, which breaks down food, and the spleen, which helps distribute the energy from food to the rest of the body. Healthy earth energy means regular bowel movements and a productive, grounded lifestyle. Someone with an earth imbalance may worry a lot and have digestive trouble. To right this ship, try meditation.

3 ✪ *Metal.* Like a conductor of electricity, metal inside the body is represented by the lungs, which takes in oxygen and sends its life-giving energy to the rest of the body, and by the large intestine, which receives and discharges waste. In China, good metal in the body doesn't mean you have a surgically implanted plate in your head or screw in your knee. It means you are organized and self-disciplined with a vital inner strength. An imbalance of metal manifests itself as sadness. A person with metal imbalance might have asthma, frequent colds, skin rashes, and chronic constipation or diarrhea. The breathing exercises of yoga are a good way to strengthen the metal element in your body.

4 ✪ *Water.* As you might imagine, the water element is related to the kidneys, which filters fluids in the body, and the bladder, which stores and discharges them. Strong water energy manifests itself in a person as fearlessness, determination, and longevity. Weak water energy on the other hand, can mean slow metabolism, urination problems, and sexual issues. The emotions associated with this imbalance are fear and anxiety. Boost the water element by, yes, drinking more water and generally staying hydrated.

5 ✪ *Wood.* Wood as it pertains to the body is realized in a healthy liver, which stores and filters blood (energy, the life giver), and the gall bladder, which stores and excretes bile. If your liver is out of whack, you might be always angry, while indecisiveness might mean something's going on with your gall bladder. Increase wood energy by laying off the booze, cutting down on fatty foods, and adding more fiber to your diet. Also, eat foods with high potassium such as seaweed.

Chinese Medicine's Yin and Yang

In Chinese medicine, yin and yang represent the opposing forces of nature. Yin is the more peaceful of the two, while yang is more fiery. When the two forces are in balance, there is a perfect opposition between the two. Just as night cannot come without day, there can be no front without a back, and joy cannot come without pain. It is also believed that a person's health is linked to his or her relationship with the world they live in. Having good relationships and being at peace with your place in the world will result in good health. Bad relationships, on the other hand, can lead to sickness.

Inside the body, if one of your interdependent Five Elements is out of balance then your yin and yang is off-kilter and there's a good chance you'll be in poor health until they are righted.

The Chinese believe that yin and yang are in constant flux, coming into and out of balance on a regular basis. The doctor is called when this balance becomes consistent and one force dominates the other more than it should. Acupuncture, massage therapy, eating right, and lifestyle changes can help rebalance your yin and yang.

Acupuncture

Acupuncture is an ancient Chinese practice that uses carefully placed needles to encourage the flow of chi, or energy, through the body. According to ancient Chinese acupuncture texts, if your chi isn't flowing right (due to bodily injury or emotional or mental stress), then your body is out of balance and you can get sick. Translation for those living in New Orleans: Your mojo ain't workin' and you got to get it back.

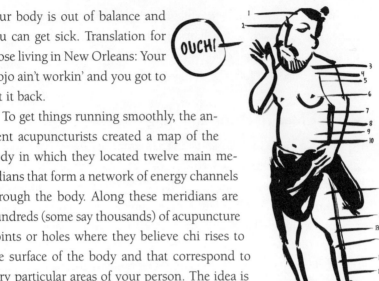

To get things running smoothly, the ancient acupuncturists created a map of the body in which they located twelve main meridians that form a network of energy channels through the body. Along these meridians are hundreds (some say thousands) of acupuncture points or holes where they believe chi rises to the surface of the body and that correspond to very particular areas of your person. The idea is to figure out what's ailing you (whether it's anxiety, acne, or a chronically sore big toe) and then stick needles in the acupuncture holes that correspond with your ailment. By doing this, you can unblock the meridians, get stagnant chi flowing again, and get your body back in balance.

Ailments and Possible Needle Placements

Should you make an appointment at an acupuncturist's office, you may be interested to know where he or she might stick you and why.

Headache—on top of the left foot between the first and second toes

Sore throat—inside right foot midway between the ankle and the top of the arch of the foot

Stiff neck—back of the right knee just inside the outer ligament

Anxiety—middle of the forehead at the hairline or middle of the abdomen just below the breastbone

Insomnia—inner side of the left wrist toward the outside of the arm

Hysteria—same placement as for insomnia

Coma—inside of pinkie finger of right hand

Vitamins and Supplements

Eating right and total enlightenment go hand in hand, but when you just can't stuff in another dark green leafy vegetable, there's always vitamin supplements. Gobbling some of these on a regular basis can give you a needed boost until you get your diet back on track.

Antioxidants

Vitamins C and E and selenium are considered antioxidants because they help neutralize harmful things in the body called free radicals. Free radicals enter our systems from muscles after we exercise, through cigarette smoke, alcohol, and drugs, and from harmful environmental pollutants. Antioxidants also strengthen the eyes, help protect the central nervous system, and keep the cardiovascular system running smoothly.

Gingko Biloba

Gingko biloba sounds like a wonder drug. It is derived from the gingko tree, which is one of the world's oldest still-living species of tree, dating back to over 150 million years. Gingko is a general brain tonic that is said to help individuals retain memory by increasing metabolism and boosting oxygen and blood flow to the brain. It's also supposed to give you more energy and relieve stress and anxiety while acting as a powerful antioxidant.

Royal Jelly

Royal jelly is not a sexual lubricant (or at least that's not its recommended use). It is in fact not very jellylike at all. This highly nutritious milky compound is manufactured by worker bees who feed it to the queen bee. Queen bees can live up to five years while worker bees die within a few weeks. Go figure. Royal jelly actually has a high amino acid content and can be a great immune system booster. Other benefits have been said to include: sexual enhancement, increased energy, weight loss, easing depression, and an intense craving for honey and flower pollen. However, if you have any known allergy to bees, stay well clear of this and all products produced by bees (including flower pollen).

Spirulina

This microscopic blue-green algae is said to be the first photosynthetic life form on the planet, producing the earth's oxygen and allowing other life-forms to evolve. By eating it you gain the knowledge of all living creatures from the beginning of time. Just kidding. Spirulina is a general tonic and antioxidant that can strengthen the immune system, improve digestive health, lower cholesterol, and help rid the body of free radicals. It's also said to help relieve bad breath, which is nice.

St. John's Wort

Also known as hypericum perforatum, St. John's Wort is normally taken as an alternative to antidepressent medication as it is thought to affect neurotransmitters in the brain in the same way. It's also good to use as a healing agent on severe wounds. In fact, the herb is named for St. John of Jerusalem, who used the herb to help patch up fallen soldiers during the Crusades.

Enlightenment Through Yoga

For the perfect enlightening balance between body, mind, and soul, yoga is the way to go. This exercise stretches the body's spine and skeletal system as well as its muscles and joints and it helps stimulate internal organs, glands, and nerves. Yoga's breathing techniques help focus and clarify the mind. Its meditation practices are a great way to get in touch with yourself and your spiritual path. In short, yoga tones the body, calms the mind, and gets you feeling focused and centered.

The history of yoga dates back to at least 3000 BCE, but it didn't appear in writing until 2500 BCE when it was written into the Hindu Upanishads as a way to unite oneself with the universe and absolute consciousness. In fact, the word yoga comes from the Sanskrit word *yogah,* which literally means "a yoking together." Even today, Hindus believe that yoga is the way you can join the ultimate consciousness of the universe. It's also a way to release vast amounts of pent-up energy through the body's seven chakra points.

Anyone with a soft spot on the ground and a room big enough to stretch out in can practice yoga. The exercise routine consists of a series of breathing techniques and asanas, or poses, that stretch the body in various ways, teaching body control and concentration of the mind. Most asanas focus on making the back and spine as supple and strong as possible, which is said to be the key to a long, happy life.

When you get started with the stretching, don't worry if you're as tight as a new drum. Things loosen up over time.

Basic Yoga Techniques

You Will Need:

Yoga mat

A quiet space, large enough to allow you to stretch your arms over your head while standing and laying flat on the ground.

Steps to Enlightenment

1 ✪ Find a comfortable spot on the ground and sit cross-legged on the ground with your back as straight as possible, so that your chest and heart feel as though they're slightly out and up. Your hands should be relaxed and in one of three positions: palms facing up with the backs of your hands placed on your thighs or knees; palms facing down on your thighs or knees; palms facing up in the same position as above except with your thumb and index finger touching in a circle. Each is meant to remind you of the reality of the moment in the here and now.

2 ✪ Breathe deeply in and out through your nose in slow but deliberate breaths. Use the diaphragm in the abdomen to completely fill your lungs and then completely empty them before taking another breath. You should be sitting up straight, but relaxed and focused on the breathing.

3 ✪ Sit and breathe for five minutes.

4 ❂ Next, lie back and prepare for the shoulder stand and plow pose. Breathing should remain deliberate and deep. In fact, throughout the exercise, focus on the calm inhale and exhale of your breathing.

5 ❂ To complete the shoulder stand from a prone position, place your hands palm down on the floor next to you as you lie flat. Breathe in and lift your feet in the air, keeping your legs straight. Then lift up your hips off the floor and bring your legs up over your head. Next, breathe out and straighten your spine. Your chin should touch your chest and your hands should be supporting your back. This pose compresses and stimulates the thyroid while making the spine flexible and stimulating blood circulation to the brain. Hold the pose for three inhales.

6 ❂ As you exhale, roll out of the shoulder stand. First lower your legs to a 45-degree angle and place your hands palm down on the floor. Then slowly roll out vertebra by vertebra until you are laying flat. Lay still for two breaths.

7 ❂ The next pose is called the cobra. Roll over on your stomach and put your feet together with your toes pointed so that the top of your feet are flat on the mat. Put your hands palm down flat on the ground just under your shoulders. Place your forehead on the ground so that you are looking toward your chest. Next, inhale and lift your head up, looking back as far as possible while pushing up with your hands and lifting your trunk off the ground. Be sure and keep your elbows in. Look back as far as possible and hold this pose for several breaths. Then push up more with your hands until your arms are straight and your torso is bending at the abdomen and your head is back, bending the neck. Don't forget to breathe. The entire spine should now be bent backward. The cobra is a back-strengthening asana. It also helps to

tone the stomach. Hold the pose in this way for several breaths before letting yourself slowly down.

8 ↻ After the Cobra comes the forward bend, one of the most important yoga asanas of them all because it stretches the back of the body from the heels to the top of the spine. Lie flat on your back, feet together, arms outstretched over your head and flat on the ground with palms together. While inhaling, raise yourself up into a sitting pose with your arms still over your head, palms still together. Continue to breathe. Your toes should be pointing slightly back toward your chest. Then bend at the waist, moving your chest slowly toward your knees and keeping your back straight. Keep going as far as possible without bending your back. Try to reach your toes with your hands. Hold the pose for at least four breaths, then roll gently back until you are lying flat on the floor.

9 ↻ At the end of every yoga session comes the corpse pose, which allows you to relax completely after stretching your body. Make sure you are lying flat (do not put your head on a pillow) and begin breathing slowly and deeply. Feel your weight and let gravity pull you into the ground into total relaxation. Relax the muscles in the face. Let the shoulders fall. Let your thighs and knees turn outward. Concentrate on how your abdomen moves up and down as you breathe. This pose allows you to release stress and preserve energy.

Word to the Wise

Always take everything very slowly with yoga. Quick moves can cause injury. Also, it's best to do yoga on an empty stomach. And be sure to wear loose-fitting clothes.

Getting the Perfect Abs Through Yoga

As we continue along our paths to total enlightenment, we should not be so taken with spiritual bliss as to neglect how we look in a bathing suit. How then would we share our newfound wisdom with interested members of the opposite sex on the beach in Goa or Thailand? Yoga is the answer. It'll give you a rock hard stomach.

You Will Need:

Yoga mat

Space to stretch out (the beach is a great place to do abdomen
    toning exercises, especially if said interested parties can see
    you working hard, sweating, etc.)

Steps to Enlightenment

1 ✪ As before any yoga session, sit cross-legged on the floor and hold your hands either palm down, palm up, or palm up with the thumb and index finger touching. Breathe deeply in and out.

2 ✪ Next, lie flat on your stomach and prepare for the cobra pose in which you will push your torso up and bend your neck backward so that the spine is completely bent and the stomach muscles are stretched and toned (see page 81 for details). To really get hard abs, separate your knees, then really drop your head back while touching your feet to the top of your head.

3 ✪ Another good abdomen pose is the bridge. Go into the shoulder stand (see page 81 for details), supporting your waist with your hands. Lower one leg to the floor closest to your butt and then the other so that your feet are flat on the floor with your knees bent. Breathe. At this point your back is arched (being supported by your hands) and your elbows are in just under your torso. Finish the pose—and this is really where the abs get a workout—by lifting one leg and then the other back into the shoulder stand. Roll out of the shoulder stand and you're done.

4 ↺ For the most intense stomach workout, try the double leg raise. Lay flat on your back, arms relaxed and slightly away from your body with the palms facing up. Inhaling, raise both legs all the way up while keeping your knees straight and your butt on the floor. Then exhale and lower your legs slowly to the floor without raising your lower back off the floor. Repeat ten times.

Word to the Wise

Your goal is a hard stomach, not a back injury. As usual, take all these exercises slowly no matter how excited you get with the thought of any upcoming dates.

Sports and Spirituality

Biologically, our bodies contain chemicals and energies that if tapped and treated right can lift us up and help us to see the light. That's why it's not only important to eat correctly and exercise (as we've seen with alternative medicine and yoga), but it's also important to push our physical selves to places we didn't think we could go. By stressing our bodies to their absolute physical end, we produce things like adrenaline and endorphins, which are naturally occurring opiate proteins that lift the spirit and relieve pain (endorphin comes from the word morphine). In other words, total enlightenment is lying dormant inside all of us and all we have to do is run ten miles or surf the big wave or jump out of an airplane to get it. Welcome to the world of sports, where physical exertion regularly takes your spirit to a higher place.

Long-Distance Running

If you ask a runner why they put themselves through so much obvious pain, the answer will always be because it makes them feel good. Not "It's good for me" or "I'm trying to impress my date." They don't say that. It's always a reference to euphoria, a state of mind known in the business as "runner's high."

That's because running is painful and pain is how your body tells you that something is wrong. To combat whatever your body thinks is wrong it will produce endorphins and that's what every runner is after.

It has been said that after running very long distances—a marathon is twenty-six miles, but there are events known as ultra-running where competitors run no less than fifty miles at a time and sometimes as much as seventy—a runner will feel as though his body no longer exists and that he is being pushed onward by his mind. Imagine, you don't even have to die to have an out-of-body experience!

You Will Need:

A good pair of running shoes
Shorts and a T-shirt
A good long route

Steps to Enlightenment

1 ✿ Running more than a few miles takes training and commitment. Running at least 26.2 miles (a marathon) takes experience. So, before you get started training, begin running a few miles a day and get some advice from a professional about technique and breathing exercises.

2 ✿ When you're ready to begin the training regimen, plan for a six-month schedule in which you will slowly increase the distance you run in three stages.

3 ✪ The first stage lasts six weeks in which you will train five days a week combining running with biking and swimming (to give your legs and knees a rest but keep your aerobic exercise going). During the first stage, start out running two miles and don't run more than five miles on any day in the first stage.

- During the third week, you shouldn't run at all.
- For weeks four, five, and six, run for two days and then take the third day off, picking back up on the fourth and fifth days. You can increase the distance you run by 10 to 15 percent on each day.

4 ✪ The next stage lasts eight weeks and the regimen is two days on, one day off, three days on, one day off, etc.

- Distances should vary between three and five miles for the first two weeks.
- Week three can include a six-mile run and by week five you should be running no less than four miles per day and no more than six.
- The final three weeks are six-mile runs every on-day.

5 ✪ The final stage should last twelve weeks with running for three days, taking a day off, then running two days before a day off, except in the last week in which you'll take it a little easier before running a marathon on the last day.

- For the first two weeks start out at eight miles for the first day and cut back to six on the rest.
- The next two weeks should start out at nine miles, cutting back to six on the rest, except on the fourth week in which you should add a ten-mile day on the fourth day on so that the week should be: Monday, nine miles, Tuesday, six miles, Wednesday, six miles, Thursday, off, Friday, ten miles, Saturday, six miles, Sunday off.

- For the next six weeks, increase the miles you run on the first day of the week by one and those you run on the fourth day on by two. Week five should look like this: Monday, ten miles, Tuesday and Wednesday, six miles, Thursday off, Friday twelve miles, Saturday six, Sunday off. By week ten you should be running fifteen miles on the first day and twenty miles on the fourth day on.
- In week eleven, cut those miles back to eight and ten respectively and in week twelve do six miles, six miles, day off, day off, two miles, and then the marathon.

Word to the Wise

Running your way into the world of enlightenment is a difficult way to go, especially considering that according to *Runner's World* magazine, 30 to 60 percent of all runners get injured every year. Take it slow and if you start to get tendonitis, shin splints, sprains, or other bone injuries the only solution is to lay off for a while.

Surfing

The notion of soul surfing got its start in the late '50s and '60s when Californian and Hawaiian surfers would glide along 4- or 5-foot-high waves on 40-pound, solid-wood, 9-foot-long boards. The idea was to see how long and how smoothly you could ride a wave before you wiped out or the wave hit the beach. For the soul surfer who is alone in the ocean swells with the sun and wind in his or her hair, riding the perfect wave to the beach is akin to becoming one with the ocean itself. For some, catching that perfect wave is no less than the meaning of life.

You Will Need:

A surfboard between 7 and 8 feet long
Board wax
Sunscreen
Wetsuit (optional)
Waves about 3 feet high
A sandy beach
Blue skies

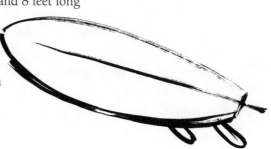

Steps to Enlightenment

1 ✪ The first thing you should do when you get to the beach is stare at the water for a good ten minutes. It's a good way to study the waves (see how big they are, where they're breaking, whether or not there are any rocks, coral, or dangerous riptides), and it's a good way to calm your mind.

2 ✪ Before hitting the surf, wax up your board, stretch your legs, and slather on some waterproof sunscreen. Riding waves may be an enlightening prospect, but having a sunburn just plain hurts.

3 ✪ Next, put your board flat on the sand and stand on it with one foot forward and one foot back. Whatever foot you naturally place toward the back of the board is your back foot and that's the one you want to attach the ankle leash to.

4 ✪ To get out to where the waves are, wait until a wave breaks on shore and then run into the water and do a kind of belly flop on your board, which should send you gliding out into the surf.

5 ✪ Lie on the center of the board (lying too far forward will cause the nose of the board to dip in the water when you're paddling out to

the waves or when you're paddling to catch a wave and that will hinder your progress). Then paddle in strong, even strokes.

6 ☯ When you come to a wave that threatens to crash on top of you and send you and your surfboard tumbling right back to the beach, do a "duck dive" by dipping the nose of the surfboard into the water and ducking your head in with it so that you go under the water (and the break) and pop up on the other side of the wave like a duck hunting for fish. This takes good timing and a fair bit of practice.

7 ☯ Paddle out to an area just past where the waves are breaking, sit up on your board, and wait.

8 ☯ When a rideable wave approaches, turn your board toward shore and paddle strongly until you feel the wave start to propel you forward.

9 ☯ Grab the sides or "rails" of the board with both hands and do a quick push up while bringing your feet underneath you, so that you end up in a squatting position with one foot in front of the other and your toes pointed toward the board's center stripe. You should still be holding onto the rails.

10 ☯ Let go of the rails and stand up, keeping your knees bent and your arms away from your body for balance.

11 ☯ Once you're up, simply follow the direction that the wave is breaking in. Keep the nose and the tail of the board from dipping too far in the water by moving your feet either to the front or the back. Control the side-to-side direction of the board by leaning in the direction you want to go.

Word to the Wise

Practice pushing up into a stand before you hit the water by laying your board flat on the sand and lying on top of it. Forget about looking silly; you don't have to look good to find spiritual enlightenment.

Parachuting

You've heard of adrenaline junkies? Well, jumping out of airplanes is their sport of choice. That's because when the body is put in this kind of perceived life-threatening peril (how is it supposed to know you're going to pull the rip cord?) the adrenal gland secretes the hormone epinephrine—better known as adrenaline—into the blood stream. This is basically your body getting ready for something bad to happen and giving it the extra blood flow and corresponding boost of energy it will need to survive.

Adrenaline causes an immediate reaction. The heart rate is increased. Pupils are dilated and glucose in the liver cells is synthesized for extra energy. Also, adrenaline redistributes blood away from the skin and inner organs, as if it were preparing for a battle. Blood vessels in the legs dilate, causing more blood to flow to muscles there in case a quick escape, rather than a confrontation, is the best option. For these reasons, the onrush of adrenaline is known as the fight-or-flight response. For parachutists the response is most definitely flight.

You Will Need:

Parachute
Airplane
Goggles
Parachute pants (not the kind from the '80s)

Steps to Enlightenment

1 ✿ Establish a target on the ground (such as a field—jumping over forests and cities is not fun).

2 ✿ Have a friend fly you no more than 12,000 feet in the air.

3 ✿ Once you get over your target and after belting out the word "Geronimo," jump headfirst out of the plane. If this is your first jump, more experienced parachutists will refer to you as a meat bomb. Try not to visualize this as you jump.

4 ✿ Free-fall at a rate of 115 to 130 miles per hour for ten seconds. During the free fall, spread arms and legs out to your side and do some general freaking out as your adrenaline tops off.

5 ✿ Pull the rip cord.

7 ✿ Pull the rip cord.

8 ✿ Pull the rip cord!

9 ✿ When your parachute opens, float peacefully to the ground, marveling at the scenery. (If your chute doesn't open, enlightenment is near. Even if it does open, enlightenment is near, so this is a win-win situation.)

10 ✿ Once on the ground, you will have achieved total enlightenment.

Word to the Wise

Find a good parachute school before going up in your friend's plane. The class will take about five hours before you can jump and it'll cost you about $125.

Part III: Soul

Confronted by the uncouth specter of old age, disease, and death,
we are thrown back upon the present, on this moment, here,
right now, for that is all there is. And surely this is the paradise of
children, that they are at rest in the present, like frogs or rabbits.

—Peter Matthiessen, *The Snow Leopard*

The third and some say the star member of the spiritual triad is, of course, the soul. It is the end result of our meditation and our yoga, the subject of our poetry, and the spot we're aiming for when we jump out of airplanes. Without soul we are incomplete. That's why if you still don't have any, you gotta get some. Soul music is a good way to do that. Also, when you do get some soul, what can you do with it? Well, you can preach, you can dance, and you can die enlightened.

Soul Music

Hey, if you're trying to get some soul, the first thing you can do is listen to some soul music. A little boogie-woogie to get the spirit movin' and the hips shakin' is as holistic as it gets. Ow! Jump back, kiss myself!

Top Ten List

1 ✪ Nina Simone, *Nina Simone Anthology*

2 ✪ Aretha Franklin, *Queen of Soul*

3 ✪ Stevie Wonder, *Songs in the Key of Life*

4 ✪ James Brown, *Get Up Offa That Thing*

5 ✪ Al Green, *Greatest Hits*

6 ✪ Barry White, *Can't Get Enough*

7 ✿ George Clinton and Parliament, *Mothership Connection*

8 ✿ Elvis Presley, *Elvis Gospel Treasury*

9 ✿ Michael Jackson, *Off the Wall*

10 ✿ Marvin Gaye, *What's Going On*

How to Become a Preacher

If you've found some soul and you have the need to show others how to get some, put on your best suit and start preaching the good word. There are two ways you can become a preacher: Attend a four-year theological college; or get right to it with a soapbox in a busy (and sinful) part of town.

You Will Need:

A soapbox, shoeshine stand, or vegetable crate
A suit and tie
Shiny shoes
Fine haircut
Bible
The movie *Wise Blood,* by John Huston
An inspiring message

Steps to Enlightenment

1 ✿ Before heading out to speak the good word to sinners everywhere, take some time to plan what you're going to say. Be sure and include lots of superlatives in the sermon such as "earth-shattering," "epic," and "forewarned." For pointers, watch the movie *Wise Blood,* about a young southern boy who decides to become a preacher to make a difference in the world.

2 ☯ When the sermon is done, read it aloud several times in front of the mirror in a forceful, convincing way. Throw in some hand-waving, body undulations, and facial distortions for the good theatrics that is the calling card of any preacher worth his salt.

3 ☯ When you've found a good spot that is obviously filled with those whose souls have not yet been made available to them or whose souls have been tainted with the devil and the devil's ways, set up your soapbox and get up on it.

4 ☯ Talk in a clear voice at a level of loudness that everyone can hear. Don't shout unless God moves you so much that you have to.

5 ☯ When a crowd has gathered, pause in places to emphasize your point and to allow the audience to laugh or say "Hallelujah!" Also, make eye contact with the crowd as a sign of trust and confidence.

6 ☯ Weeping is acceptable. Be sure and bend your knees.

7 ☯ After your speech is done, let everyone know that they, too, can find total enlightenment through the word of God.

Word to the Wise

Bring a handkerchief to daub sweat from your brow during the sermon.

How to Get Saved

Are you having trouble finding some soul or, as is the case more often than people realize, have you found your soul only to lose it? If so, there's a good chance you will have found yourself at the end of your tether or at rock bottom and in a world of misery where there's nowhere else to turn and you simply don't know how to deal with the difficulties you face. That's good. It's the first place you need to go to get saved.

You Will Need:

To hit rock bottom
The will to find enlightenment

Steps to Enlightenment

1 ↻ The first step to saving yourself is to admit that you are powerless to do anything about it. There may be much crying at this stage, which is fine. Only when you really feel the pain are you ready to be saved.

2 ↻ The second step is to look for something larger than yourself for help. This can be a god of your choice or a higher power of any kind, but it can also be an idea or a philosophy from someone who has been through what you're now going through.

3 ↻ That brings us to the third step, which is to seek out others who can help. Twelve-step programs, church congregations, yoga classes, and the beaches of Thailand can all be good places to relate to people who might also be lost or searching for lost souls. More importantly, these groups can give you practical tools to help you get on and stay on the path to enlightenment.

4 ↻ Once you've completed steps 1 to 3, keep on practicing what you've learned. Getting saved is the first step in a long life of staying saved and that takes work.

Word to the Wise

Getting saved is not a far-off eventuality that might happen to you when you die or only after you give homage to some god or another. It's a real possibility that you can achieve on any given day, because the beauty of the soul is that it is always longing to lift us up. We just have to let it.

Ecstatic Dancing:
Basic Techniques of the Whirling Dervish

"To God belong the East and the West,
and wherever you turn is the face of God."

—Koran, chapter 2, verse 115

Contrary to what some people may think, the Whirling Dervishes of Turkey do not spin around and around for hours on end just to see how dizzy they can get. They may have done that as kids, after which they would fall to the ground in fits of giggles as their parents warned them that they'd stay that way forever if they didn't quit it. But not anymore. Now, they spin as part of a seven-hundred-year-old Sufi tradition of surrendering themselves to Allah through ecstatic dancing.

The idea of getting closer to God by losing yourself in a dance number isn't a new one. Tribal shamans have been doing it around the world for centuries as have Hindus, Catholics, and various other organized and unorganized religions. The Baptists, of course, do not dance, but that's because they'll go straight to burning hell if they do. But for those who do dance for enlightenment, the concept has to do with forfeiting yourself—your ego, your worries, your hang-ups, every-thing—to the ecstasy of the movement so that once you lose control of all thought you achieve rapture and are transported into the realm of the divine. In other words, when you dance, be it whirling, two-stepping, or bumpin' and grindin', you are living squarely in the moment.

You Will Need:

A tall white hat made out of a seamless piece of camel's hair
    double-ply felt
A wide white skirt
Large space or dance floor
Quick feet
Stout constitution

Dance Steps to Enlightenment

1 ✿ First, clear away the furniture or, better yet, go outside. First-time whirlers tend to whirl all over the place before getting the swing of things, so to speak.

2 ✿ Then get dressed in the camel's hair hat and the white skirt. The hat represents the tombstone of the ego and the skirt the ego's burial veil— don't forget: This dance is all about giving yourself up.

3 ✿ Before any dance, dervishes begin by striking a pose called an *alif* in which they cross their arms with each hand resting on an opposite shoulder.

4 ✿ Staying in the *alif* pose, bow deeply and then come back up. This symbolizes that the dancer is ready to surrender him or herself.

5 ✿ Now you're ready to start spinning. Stand with legs slightly apart and knees bent. Unfold your arms from the *alif* pose and open them up as if you're about to give the world a big hug. Then raise the right arm up at your side to a 45-degree angle and turn your right palm to the sky as if to receive God. The left arm should extend parallel to the floor with the palm turned down as if to channel God to the earth and into the world.

6 ↻ Turn your head to the left and stare at your left hand. The eyes should remain on your left hand at all times.

7 ↻ Now, use your left leg as an axis and push off the ground with your right leg, which crosses behind the left leg and comes down in the same spot it pushed off from. The goal is to make a 360-degree turn with each movement. Once you get the hang of it you can pick up speed so that you get into a steady rhythm. The key to balance is to place yourself into a meditative state and to concentrate on your innermost core. In other words, concentrate on centering yourself.

8 ↻ Ideally, spinning should last forty minutes, but it takes months of practice to attain this kind of stamina and concentration.

9 ↻ When you're done spinning, come to rest in another *alif* pose.

How to Be

*"The struggle itself towards the heights
is enough to fill a man's heart."*

—Albert Camus

Be in the now. Carpe diem. Live for the moment. If there is a New Age mantra then this is it, adopted from Eastern religious movements like Buddhism and co-opted by baby boomer divorcees to cope with only getting to be a part of their children's lives *some* of the time. And indeed there is some life-nurturing and even spiritual merit to the philosophy of being who you are without worrying about the past or looking toward the future.

But how does one become exactly who they are? The Existentialists like Sartre and Camus said that we are what we can become. For that reason, they thought that the now wasn't as relevant as the future, which is where all our becoming will end up. Regardless, existentialism asserts that we can become who we are by making choices. Not any old choices, mind you, but life choices that are made in good faith to yourself. If you really want to become an archaeologist, for example, but you choose to be a lawyer instead, then that decision could be argued as being made in bad faith. The result of that, of course, is angst, which is what happens when you start to doubt your choices.

So in reality becoming who you are may be a combination of making choices in good faith and being able to be present enough in the now to see those choices through while enjoying what you do while you're doing it.

Right Versus Wrong Choices

Wrong choice: You drink far too much at your best friend's wedding and end up flirting with his mother and hurling on the gift table.

Right choice: You drink far too much but have the sense to leave before making a fool of yourself.

Wrong choice: You are gay but you choose to marry and have kids with a member of the opposite sex, thereby suppressing your true self and dragging someone else into the lie with you.

Right choice: You are gay and decide to come out to your parents before they find your love letters to your childhood friend, Johnny (or Janie, whatever the case may be).

Wrong choice: You wear white pants after Labor Day.

Right choice: You keep up with the latest fashions.

Wrong choice: Someone you don't find attractive in any way whatsoever asks you out on a date and you say, "Sure, I'd love to."

Right choice: When that person asks you out, you find the self-confidence to be honest and say no.

Wrong choice: You have an opportunity to pursue your dreams but fear and cynical words from others become your reasons for not going for it.

Right choice: When the opportunity to follow your dreams comes up, you realize that it's going to be a little scary and that there's a chance for failure, but you decide to do it anyway, even if you fail, because trying and failing is always better than not trying at all.

Total Enlightenment Through Death

"There is no me after death.
Therefore, there is nothing to fear in death itself.
It is a returning to the non-me."

—Arthur Dobrin, *Spiritual Timber*

The Greek philosopher Epicurus pointed out that we never really consider not having existed before we were born. It's only the part about not existing after we die that keeps us up at night. Yet, why should one be so much more horrible than the other?

The great thing about dying is that it is a part of living and to live life to its fullest we must also die. Still, there's something about death that most folks find a little daunting.

To certain degree, the prospect of death is why religions and the idea of God and God myths were created in the first place; they were a way to stave off panic and fright by explaining one of life's great mysteries. In the Christian, Jewish, and Islamic religions, death is what happens before you go to heaven (or hell, for those who didn't live "right"). Hindus and Buddhists think that death is just the beginning to a new life based on the karma you banked in the last one. Had religion not addressed the subject of death, the idea that when we die our souls would enter into a bottomless black meaningless void for eternity would have scared the pants off everyone and nothing would have gotten done. I mean, what's the point of life if death is one big nothing?

But viewing death through the prism of a religion isn't necessarily the best way to deal with dying and it may not be the best way to total enlightenment.

Consider the fact that being scared of death is a control issue. We don't want to die or we deny death because that means we have to give up control of life. Then again, maybe we fear death because we're egomaniacs and when we die we are robbed of ourselves, or, as Arthur Dobrin points out, we return to the "non-me." Either way, if we're so wrapped up in ourselves, then we're not paying attention to the greater notion of how we belong to the universe. And that means neither can we know who we are nor can we meet the end of our journey with grace and meaning.

The fact is, most people don't ever think about death until they get sick or almost die or a family member almost dies. And only then do they realize that death is real and they set out to savor every minute of life until they too must meet their end. Herein lies the key to enlightenment through death. If we think about our own deaths on a daily basis, then our lives will be that much richer. We will feel a larger connection to the universe and a greater commitment to discovering who we are. As Jean-Paul Sartre and the existentialists pointed out: Only when we are aroused by our own deaths will the potential of our lives become known to us.

We wanderers, ever seeking the lonelier way, begin no day where we have ended another day, and no sunrise finds us where sunset left us. Even while the earth sleeps we travel. We are the seeds of the tenacious plant, and it is in our ripeness and our fullness of heart that we are given to the wind and are scattered.

—KAHLIL GIBRAN, *The Prophet*

c h a p t e r

THREE

Wandering in the Wilderness

The Native Americans called wandering a vision quest, while the Buddha thought it would help him overcome suffering. Jesus and Mohammad wandered too, either because they wanted to tempt their faiths or because they were on the run. These days, young people wander around the world behind the wheel of a car or with backpacks hanging off their shoulders for no reason but to see the world (and perhaps themselves in the bargain). So what's with all the wandering? Well, for one thing, it's fun. For another, it's a challenge that usually ends up as a spiritual awakening. The fact is, when we leave home in search of greater goals and we separate ourselves from the things that are familiar to us, we see the world and ourselves in the world as they truly are. And that, my friends, is nothing short of total enlightenment.

Wilderness Survival

When they left Egypt, most of the Jews that Moses freed wandered in the wilderness for forty days and forty nights looking for the Promised

Land. Unfortunately, most of them kicked the bucket, because according to the Bible they whined too much and God got really sick of it and wouldn't show them the way. Had they known some basic desert survival skills, they probably could've lasted a little longer (and maybe even set up their own Promised Land, albeit a godless one). So if you're going to be doing any amount of wandering in wilderness areas—either deserts or forests—go prepared.

Basic Wilderness Survival Kit

1 ✿ Standard first aid kit

2 ✿ Pocket knife

3 ✿ Compass

4 ✿ Lighter

5 ✿ Candle

6 ✿ Whistle (for calling for help and frightening off bears)

7 ✿ Mirror (for signaling airplanes and other passing vehicles)

8 ✿ Water purification tablets

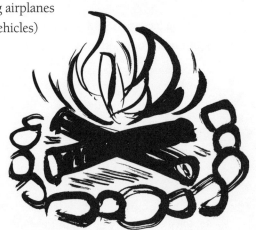

9 ✿ Canteen

10 ✿ Sewing kit

11 ✿ Fishing line

12 ✿ Hooks

13 ✿ Medical blanket

Foraging for Food and Water in the Woods

Humans can last up to ten days without food, but a day or two without water is not a good idea. Luckily, there are all kinds of yummy plants and insects to eat in the forest and water is fairly easy to find. If you just can't find anything to drink, consider partaking of your own urine. It's not very enlightening, at least not in a good way, and this won't be the story you tell your friends once they find you. However, humans have been known to survive for many days with urine, even though it has a high saline content (though not as much as seawater). Just know that you can't keep urine overnight; it goes bad.

Finding water

You Will Need:

Your canteen
A cloth (shirts or triangle bandages will work)
Knife or machete
Water purification tablets or a fire to boil the water

Steps to Enlightenment

1 ✿ Look for rainwater collected in trees, rock crevices, or large leaves. If you can't dip it out with your canteen or hand, use a cloth to soak the water up and then wring out your cloth over a canteen.

2 ✿ Purify any water you collect with purification tablets or by boiling it for three to five minutes.

3 ✿ Bamboo stalks also collect water. Simply bend them over to drain the water out.

4 ✿ Snow and ice should be melted first before drinking. When frozen, these can lower your body temperature and cause diarrhea—two things you don't want when wandering anywhere, much less in the wilderness.

5 ✿ If you happen to be wandering in tropical wildernesses near beaches (which are popular for wanderers and seekers of all ages), look for banana trees. If you cut the tree off about six inches above the ground and dig out a bowl in the stump, water from the tree's roots will collect there.

Finding food

The two things you want to watch out for with food you find outside are that it's a) not festering with maggots and b) not poisonous. Poisoning yourself would seriously hinder your search for total enlightenment.

Things to steer clear of include mushrooms of any kind, anything that is the color red, berries (unless you're absolutely sure you know what it is), bright caterpillars, dead insects, five-segmented fruit, and anything that tastes bitter or gives a burning sensation, as well as anything that smells like almonds (what you're smelling is cyanide). So, as long as you don't stuff in anything bad, you should have no problem wandering around in the wilderness finding your soul for a few weeks.

Good things to eat include the following:

1 ✿ Algae, moss, and lichens. These plants are high in protein and contain antioxidants and immune system boosters. If you find some, wash them in fresh water and boil them into a jelly.

2 ✿ Nuts. These are another good source of protein. They're usually hard to find.

3 ✪ Grasshoppers, crickets, termites, fly larvae, grubs, slugs, maggots, and worms. Yes, they're gross, but wanderers cannot be choosers. Look under logs, on dead animals, and in swampy areas around water.

4 ✪ Moths and caterpillars. Try roasting these babies.

5 ✪ Dandelions. It's possible to eat the flower, leaf, and root of this plant.

6 ✪ Bark. The inner bark of pine and birch trees is soft and chewy.

7 ✪ Pine needles. You can make good tea with these.

Desert Survival

Surviving in the desert is different than making a go of it in the forest. You are much more exposed to the elements in wide open spaces and there is a very real risk of sunburn, sunstroke, and severe dehydration. Water is doubly important and, of course, much more scarce, though it's out there. If you know your searching will take you to a desert, take along a basic survival kit (mentioned earlier), but add a few of the extras mentioned below. Then if you get lost on your wandering, here's what to do.

You Will Need:

Sunglasses
Large-brimmed hat that will stay on your head in the wind
Lightweight long-sleeve shirts and pants
One gallon of water per day per person

Steps to Enlightenment

1 ✪ Water is always a top concern in the desert. First off, a good way to prevent dehydration is to avoid working, wandering, and sweating during the hottest time of the day. It's best to find some shade (more on this later) and rest. Doing activities in the early morning or at night is key to your survival.

2 ✷ Look for water by noticing the direction birds fly in or by heading toward green plants. Cactus plants, especially the tall cylindrical barrel cacti, are great sources of water. Just cut the cactus open and squeeze out the liquid, taking care in your haste not to get stuck. Also, try digging on the banks of dry creek beds to find water.

3 ✷ Anytime you feel thirsty, you should take a big gulp of water rather than a sip, which isn't enough to do anything.

4 ✷ Fire is another big concern. It can get cold in the desert at night. Plus, a fire can be used to cook food and as a signal.

5 ✷ It's very important to stay out of the sun in the desert as much as possible to conserve the body's water content. To create shelter, drape a sleeping bag over a low bush or use leafy branches to create a tepee. Most desert survivalists will also tell you not to sit directly on the ground, which gets warmed up by the sun and can heat your body up quickly.

6 ✷ Finding food in the desert isn't easy and it really isn't the biggest concern. In fact, the more you eat in a hot climate, the more water your body will require.

Word to the Wise

The real key to any survival experience is staying calm and collected. Most injuries and fatalities happen when people who get lost in the desert (or anywhere, for that matter) begin to panic. They run off cliffs, attract the attention of wildlife, and generally use up the valuable strength and energy they'll need to make it out with their souls still in their bodies.

Taking a Pilgrimage

Make real your quest for enlightenment by committing to one of the thousands of pilgrimages that take place every year all over the world. Not only will you find other pilgrims to share your questions with, but you'll find plenty of time to ponder your path as you walk through foreign countrysides with other seekers.

What to Bring

In general, most spiritualists and religions eschew material stuff for the stuff of the soul, which is to say you don't need much of anything when you go on a pilgrimage. The most stark example of this is illustrated at the Kumbh Mela, a Hindu gathering, where a group of holy men known as the Naga Babas show up totally naked. Now that's faith! Most of the rest of us should wear at least a hair shirt, sackcloth or some kind of modest dress (if you go to Mecca for the Islamic pilgrimage, you'll need to wear something white). Indeed, showing up in your birthday suit to Canterbury Cathedral will likely send you on a pilgrimage to the local jail.

Otherwise, take a really good pair of walking or running shoes, especially for multiday walking treks like those to Santiago de Compostela in Spain. Leather sandals like those worn by Jesus or no shoes at all will not make the holy trek more holy unless pain and blisters are part of your spiritual thing. Power bars and lots of liquids are essential, as are a good inspirational book (such as this one) and a journal. Remember, the need for mind-body-soul balance is the key to life's search.

Also, bring a good guidebook for the country you're going to. After the pilgrimage, there might be a good beach nearby on which to sit and ponder your newfound enlightenment.

A List of Some of the World's Most Enlightening Places

The reason to take a pilgrimage can range from religious necessity to spiritual desire. It's also a novel way to travel; you get to see off-the-beaten-track places while experiencing local customs. So when you're deciding where to go, it's important to consider your spiritual goals as well as what you want to see. Are you there to learn about a religion or talk to others with similar faiths about their viewpoints? Do you want spiritual inspiration or worldly experience? Whatever the case, enlightenment is sure to follow close behind.

Kumbh Mela Festival: Haridwar, Ujjain, Nasik, and Prayag, India

This Hindu pilgrimage and festival is the largest spiritual gathering on the planet with some fifteen million people making the trip (good luck finding a hotel room). It celebrates the alignment of the planet Jupiter as it enters Aquarius and the sun as it enters Aries. The event takes place in twelve-year cycles with meetings every four years in one of four Indian cities. It reaches its most epic proportions every twelfth year at Prayag, the confluence of the three sacred rivers of India—the Ganges, the Yamuna, and the Saraswati. Pilgrims come to bathe in the rivers and by doing so their sins are washed away and they gain total liberation.

Varanasi, India

This city on the banks of the sacred Ganges River is both a major Hindu religious center and a popular backpackers' destination. The Hindus come to bathe in the river (which is unbelievably putrid and polluted) and it is believed that if you die here you will reach instant enlightenment. Many who die elsewhere have their cremated ashes sprinkled in the Ganges here. The backpackers that come here find a unique Indian cultural experience along with easygoing but highly spiritual attitudes and cheap rent.

Canterbury Cathedral, Canterbury, England

This is the building inside which Saint Thomas Becket was murdered by four unknown knights acting in supposed allegiance to England's King Henry II. His death quickly became a rallying cry for Christians in and around Europe, many of whom flocked to the church to be near his death and reaffirm their faith. Today, more than a million pilgrims visit the church and Becket's tomb each year. A candle stays lit in the very spot where he was killed.

Uluru or Ayers Rock, Australia

Uluru is the Australian aboriginal name given to this massive red hunk of sandstone marking the open plains in the center of the Australian outback. They believe that the rock is the meeting point of many different dream lines, the ancient aboriginal pathways established many thousands of years ago by previous generations. The base of the round rock is six miles around and it is two miles long and about 1,200 feet high, making it the largest monolith in the world. About 500,000 people a year visit the site to witness the sunset and to take in the rock's special spiritual gravity.

Mecca, Saudi Arabia

The pilgrimage to Mecca is considered by Muslims as one of the five pillars of Islam. In other words, if you're Muslim you're expected to go. If you're not a Muslim, then you're better off checking into another journey as non-Muslims aren't allowed in. Sheesh, talk about uptight! Anyway, millions of Muslim pilgrims make the trip every year. They congregate at the Ka'ba, a black cube-shaped stone building, for prayers and fellowship. They also do various other rites such as visiting the Mount of Mercy, which is where Mohammad supposedly gave his Farewell Sermon.

Santiago de Compostela, Spain

This small town in the Pyrenees mountains that form the border between Spain and France became a Catholic pilgrimage site after the remains of the Apostle Santiago were discovered here in the ninth century. The most dedicated pilgrims make the thirty-day hike from France along the Way of St. James because they believe it will cut their stay in purgatory down by half. Others go to witness the gorgeous European countryside and to get a certificate of pilgrimage so they can get three nights' free accommodation and three free meals at the Hotel de Los Reyes.

Bodh Gaya and Sarnath, India, and Kusingara and Lumbini, Nepal

These four villages in Northern India and Southern Nepal are all Buddhist pilgrim centers based around the life, teachings, and death of the Buddha. Each one is fairly close to the other, making this an all-inclusive pilgrimage. Siddhartha Gautama is believed to have been born in Lumbini. He discovered enlightenment at the bodhi tree in Bodh Gaya. He first preached about the Four Noble Truths at Sarnath. Kusingara is where he is believed to have died.

Graceland, Memphis, Tennessee

Graceland is the home and final resting place of Elvis, the King of Rock and Roll. Come see mid to late '70s décor at its most outlandish and pay your respects to his Hugeness.

Mount Kailas, Tibet, China

This remote Tibetan mountain is considered by Buddhists, Hindus, Jains, and followers of the ancient Bon religion of Tibet to be the most sacred site in all of Asia. Some say that just *getting* to the mountain is a tough, taxing pilgrimage, never mind the thirty-two-mile trek around its base that is the *actual* pilgrimage. By walking clockwise around this mountain pilgrims can cause all sins to disappear.

Sri Pada or Adam's Peak, Sri Lanka

Shared by Buddhists, Hindus, Muslims, and Christians as a sacred site, the temple at the top of this mountain contains a large footprint said to belong to either the Buddha, Shiva, Adam, or St. Thomas, depending on what religion you practice.

Bethlehem and Jerusalem, Israel

Bethlehem is held in high regard by Christians as the birthplace of Jesus. Jerusalem is one of the holiest sites in the world for Christians, Jews, and Muslims. By visiting the town and its various temples and mosques, followers of these religions can pray and reinvigorate their faiths.

First, there is the Temple Mount, the location that Jews believe is the site of the First and Second Temples of Judaism, the last of which was destroyed in 70 CE. They believe this is where redemption will occur when the Messiah arrives. The last remaining wall of the temple is called the Western Wall and it is the holiest site in Judaism, where Jews come to pray.

To complicate things and add tension, the Western Wall is also part of a larger wall that encloses what Muslims call the Haram al-Sharif or the Noble Sanctuary. It is one of the three most sacred sites in that religion. Inside the sanctuary is Dome of the Rock, the spot from which Muhammad ascended into heaven, and the al-Aksa mosque, the original site where all Muslims came to pray (it is now Mecca).

Christians believe that Jerusalem's Old City holds the Holy Sepulchre, in which Jesus was buried, and from which he returned from the dead.

Long-Distance Walking Tips and Techniques

If you're planning a real pilgrimage, then there's going to be some walking in your future, maybe lots of it. For that reason, it's essential to start exercising and training in advance, especially if you'll be carrying a pack. Walking is great for the body's cardiovascular system as well as the lungs. If you go long distances, it won't be anywhere close to running a marathon, but it can take its toll on leg muscles and ligaments that aren't used to so much use. Training breaks in new shoes and tones parts of your body you'll be using the most. Following are some tips to remember before you go and while you're walking.

1 ✿ Before you start training, get out a topographical map and take a look at the route your pilgrimage will take. Note steep inclines as well as off-road paths or sidewalks. Also, be sure and find out what the weather will be like during the time of year the pilgrimage is taking place. You'll want to know if you'll be walking in sunshine or shade. When you know these things, try to mimic the terrain on training walks (if you live in Kansas and your pilgrimage is in the Himalayas, then do the best you can).

2 ✿ Buy some good shoes. If the pilgrimage is on well worn and established trails, consider getting some lightweight but supportive running shoes. Shoe salesmen say that the best running shoes should be able to go between 350 and 550 miles before blowing out. If your trail will include some rough off-road hiking, then consider a lightweight hiking boot with ankle support and a really good shock absorbent insole. In either case, you'll need to walk about one hundred miles in these new shoes to break them in.

3 ✿ For training walks, be sure and carry the pack and the contents of the pack you're going to bring. This helps get you used to having weight on your back. It'll also help dissuade you from packing too much.

4 ✿ When training, focus on endurance and rest. Walking twenty-five miles in eight hours or less is not an unreasonable goal. To get to that level, though, you'll need to start training at least three months in advance. Start out with three to five miles a day every other day for the first week and increase your mileage incrementally for each week after that. How fast you go is not important, and in fact, the longer the walk the slower you should go. Focus instead on a consistent pace. Also, be sure and rest between walking days to allow your muscles and body to recoup and build up energy.

5 ✿ During the pilgrimage, walk with your head high, shoulders relaxed, and stomach in. Also, don't let your arms just hang at your sides. Let them swing forward and backward to keep circulation flowing.

6 ✿ Don't forget to stretch before and after each day's walk.

Treating blisters

Blisters are to walking like ketchup is to French fries: You don't have to get it, but most of the time you do. Prevent blisters by trying out what works best for you during training. Professional long-distance walkers suggest buying socks that wick moisture away from your skin. Others say a double layer of socks is the best. Some even recommend changing socks twice a day. If you think you're getting a blister—you'll feel a "hot spot" on the skin—stop walking immediately and put some breathable first aid tape or blister pads over it before hitting the trail again. If you do get a blister, here's what to do.

You Will Need:

Moleskin or some kind of "second skin"
First aid tape

Steps to Enlightenment

1 ✿ Do not pop the blister. This will leave it vulnerable to dirt and infection.

2 ✿ Most blister moleskins already come in the shape of a doughnut—round with a hole cut out in the middle. If not, cut yours in this shape to fit around your blister. Stick the moleskin to your foot with the blister poking up through the hole.

3 ✿ Use breathable first aid tape to secure the moleskin in place and gently cover the blister.

Word to the Wise

If you happen to be walking next to cold streams, soaking your feet in the water at each rest stop will cool down feet and keep blisters away.

The Road Trip

Ah, the road trip: wind in your hair, tunes blaring, freedom welling up inside your youthful soul, and a direction to nowhere but the long open road to adventure. This recipe for enlightenment is yours for the taking.

But first, you must plan. Either that or risk traveling thousands of miles with someone you can't stand or traveling only so far as the gas in your tank will take you because you don't have any more money to fill up. Neither option is going to set your soul on fire.

Going Solo or Tandem

The first question you should ask yourself is should you take this road trip alone or with someone. There are good and bad sides to each argument.

Going solo means you get to make all the decisions on where to go and when (depending on what strikes your fancy). Plus, you're more open to meeting new people. Traveling in groups tends to insulate you from the culture you're traveling through. Also, if you're focused on finding yourself (i.e., enlightenment), being alone might be the best way to explore your soul and its place in the world. Friends, especially ones you've known a long time, could keep you in the comfort zone you're yearning to break out of and they could balk at any changes they see happening to you.

That said, inviting a friend along allows you to live your experiences with someone else and inject some always-helpful humor into the journey. You'll be able to share traveling expenses on both gas and hotel rooms. Road trip buddies can also lend courage to the expedition that can push you in ways and places that you might not have explored on your own.

If you do decide to go with someone other than yourself, be sure you know what you're getting into. If your friend is shy and careful, then they're not going to give you courage. Someone too opinionated and talkative isn't going to give you the space you need to stretch your wings. Whoever you choose, just make sure they have some personality traits that are different from yours so that you complement each other. Also, make sure you and this person will have lots to talk about and that he or she won't feel uncomfortable if there's no talking at all. Your individual paths to enlightenment must eventually be your own, but if you can share a path for a small amount of time, there's nothing wrong with achieving total enlightenment together.

Planning Before You Go

1 ✿ Get a map of the country you're planning on road-tripping in and plot your route knowing full well that the route will be changed, augmented, and abbreviated many, many times along the way.

2 ✿ Figure out how much money you'll need by first venturing a rough guess on how long you'll be gone and how far you'll go. Think about hotel or camping costs, daily food rations, and roadside kitsch you'll want to bring home. Then bring a little extra.

3 ✿ To determine fuel costs, divide the total miles you're planning to drive by the fuel efficiency of your car (i.e., how many miles per gallon do you get?). Then multiply that number by the average cost of a gallon of gas where you're traveling.

4 ✿ Make sure the car is in good working order. Consider getting new tires. Check all fluids and give it a tune-up.

5 ✪ Get yourself an ice chest and stock it with good snacks and drinks. You'll have to replenish the ice as you go, but that's definitely preferable to Stuckey's, Cracker Barrel, or any other local shop that sells hockey pucks and lard disguised as "home cooking."

6 ✪ Watch *Fandango,* a great road trip movie.

7 ✪ Read *On the Road,* the greatest road trip book of them all.

Road Trip Protocol

Road-tripping may be a good enlightening time, but not if the person you're in a car with for most of each day insists on eating beans at every meal. In order to find total enlightenment on a road trip, you and your partner are going to have to follow a few simple rules of engagement.

1 ✪ Don't talk too much.

2 ✪ Don't ask to pull over and go to the bathroom every fifteen minutes.

3 ✪ Do ask the other person in the car what music they want to listen to, if at all.

4 ✪ Don't fart, poot, pass wind, or in any way emit gaseous clouds from your bottom.

5 ✪ Do take turns driving.

6 ✪ Do drive safely when it is your turn, especially if it's not your car.

7 ✪ Do stop when the other person sees something of interest, wants to snap a photo, or just have a look around. After all, enlightenment cannot be found in cars alone.

Where to Find a Wise Man on a Mountain

A Fable

After days of precipitous climbing and cold nights, the young boy rounded a bend to find an old bearded man dressed in robes and sitting cross-legged on a high precipice as if in meditation.

"What is the meaning of life?" the boy asked breathlessly.

The old man looked at the boy's tattered, blistered feet and his tired eyes.

"You have been searching this mountain for a long time," he said. "But to find the answer to your question, you must sit still and search inside yourself."

At this the boy fell down in exhaustion and wept.

"You mean I didn't have to climb all this way? I nearly froze to death," he said. "I fended off wild animals and ate berries and leaves to survive. Once, I nearly fell off a cliff to my death. And now you're telling me I could have stayed home?"

"I told you no such thing!" said the wise man.

If, during your search for enlightenment, you've blown a tire, stubbed a toe, or simply pooped out and can go no further, it might be time to get some sage advice. For that you need look no further than the local wise man, who has no doubt chosen the very top of the tallest mountain in town to call home. Wise men

go for the hermetic, minimalist seclusion of the mountains because there they don't have to deal with all the dummies down below who keep bugging them with silly questions like what color should I paint my house or is it better to lease a car or finance a new one? For a wise man, life is always a case of being the smartest one at the dinner table but still having to make small talk about the salmon mousse. So they head for the hills, the idea being that if you want some advice or some answers, you're going to have to work hard to get them, and even then it's not guaranteed. These wise guys are so private that if they see you coming, they'll try to avoid you. Here's how to find what you're looking for.

Steps to Enlightenment

1 ✪ Wise men are loath to perch atop anything under twelve thousand feet, so the best place to go find one is in the Nepalese Himalayas, where the smallest mountains reach fourteen thousand feet and where eight of the world's ten tallest mountains exist, including Mount Everest (whose tenant, by the way, moved to a neighboring peak several years back because of the excessive traffic).

2 ✪ Wise men sit and meditate for most of the day so if you listen for chants of OM or other similar sounds, there's a chance you'll be able to sneak up on the old fella while he's in a trance. If you do that though, try not to scare him so much that he has a heart attack and dies. It's bad karma to kill a wise man and plain bad luck to go all that way and not get the answer to the meaning of life.

3 ✪ If you think you're getting close, look for evidence of human existence like toilet paper. Even though wise men have lofty thoughts, they still have to shit like the rest of us.

4 ✪ Beware wise-man imposters who talk a fast talk but give out lousy advice such as "life's a bitch."

5 ✿ The Nepalese believe that the yeti—or the Abominable Snow-man—exists in the higher altitudes of the Himalayas, so in your search for the meaning of life, don't mistake a hairy white apelike figure for a haggard skinny wise man. You'll get no answers there.

Word to the Wise

Pain, hunger, and general suffering are all part of the search for wisdom, so if you think you've had enough, expect a little more and know that the wise man is most assuredly around the next bend.

Mountain-Climbing Techniques

Before you set out on your search for mountain-based wisdom, get yourself acquainted with tents, climbing skills, good boots, and warm clothes. No one ever said that too much gear is going to get in the way of total enlightenment.

You Will Need:

Outdoor survival kit
Medium to heavyweight hiking boots with ankle support
A four-season tent with snow flaps and tie-down straps
Below-freezing–grade down sleeping bag
Two sets of warm lightweight clothing
Camping stove
Food that is high in carbohydrates
Lots of water
Optional: Climbing rope, harness, crampons, ice axe

Steps to Enlightenment

1 ✿ Plan out your ascent and plan to stop at 8,000 feet above sea level for at least a full day to acclimatize to the thinner air and avoid altitude sickness. Go between 1,000 and 1,500 feet a day after that (climbing more is unwise and if you meet a wise man, he'll tell you just that). Give yourself plenty of daylight time at the end of each day to set up camp for the night.

2 ✿ Like long-distance walking, it doesn't matter how fast you climb a mountain as much as it does how steadily you go. Keep an even pace, resting as often as you like, but stick to well-marked trails. Wise men may be hard to find but they have to get food and water some way, which means some hired lacky is walking up and down the mountain wearing a pretty good trail.

3 ✿ Once you're above 8,000 feet and your body is working hard to get used to the high altitudes, walk slowly and drink plenty of water to help offset altitude sickness.

4 ✿ Watch out for avalanches and falling rocks. When crossing an avalanche field, walk quickly but not so quick that you'll lose your footing. Do not stop—even for a minute—in an area where there's been a recent avalanche.

5 ✿ When you stop for the night, pitch your tent. Then take off the sweaty clothes you hiked in and put on the second, drier (and warmer) pair you have in your pack. Change back into the first pair for the next day's trek. It'll be cold and miserable, but it's nothing compared to never having a dry pair of clothes to change into.

Word to the Wise

If you are having trouble breathing or sleeping at high altitudes or if you are lightheaded, nauseous, or vomiting you may have altitude sickness. Descend to at least 1,000 feet right away and stay there to acclimatize for twenty-four hours.

The whole experience was an opening up of the soul and spirit for me. . . . I was hooked, and for life, as it has turned out. . . . I was a late bloomer who was still growing up. I didn't get started on life until I was about thirty-two, which was good because I was old enough to appreciate it. I had it all ahead of me.

—CHEF JULIA CHILD,
recalling dining on her first French meal of oysters
on the half shell, a green salad, filet of sole in butter
and lemon, crème fraîche, a bottle of Pouilly-Fuissé,
and a cup of strong coffee in 1948 in Rouen, France.

c h a p t e r
FOUR
Enlightenment Through Eating

Eating (or not eating at all) has been part of the path to enlightenment for centuries, whether you're a Catholic taking communion at Mass or a Buddhist monk fasting in a cave for heightened spiritual awareness. But let's set religion aside for the moment and remember how high we feel after a meal at the finest French restaurant in town, where only the freshest vegetables and the most exotic and delectable meats are served by waiters who treat us like gods or kings and queens for a night. Come to think of it, cooking itself can brighten the soul, especially if you're drinking wine with good friends while chopping up the evening's basil. In a way, it's a little like mixing potions (and for those mixing up a chocolate cake, a love potion). Then when it comes time for the big feast, everyone sits around a big table savoring food and life together in one big meaningful ritual. Forget the fast food. Spiritual dining is slow, deliberate and—let's not forget—tasty.

How to Take Communion

The Christian and especially Catholic ceremony of taking communion (also known as Mass or the Eucharist), represents in most churches a reenactment of when Jesus broke bread with his disciples and passed around a cup of wine at the Last Supper. Talk about a totally enlightening meal! According to the Bible, Jesus passed around some bread and said, "Try some of this, fellas. This is my body, which is given to you, but it won't hurt me if you bite. Do this in remembrance of me."

Some churches have taken this quite literally and actually believe that the blessed wafers or bits of bread they pass out to their congregations really are the body of Christ and that the thimbles full of screw-top wine they offer really is the blood of Christ. This means that if there's any of Christ's body or blood left over after everyone has taken communion, it's not uncommon to see the priest stuffing in the rest of it. He can't rightly put Christ in the garbage disposal now can he?

Regardless, taking part in this most enlightening of food experiences is done in a very particular way.

You Will Need:

A modest appearance (to show respect)
Knowledge of how to hold out your hands or open your mouth
    with tongue slightly out

Steps to Enlightenment

1 ✪ Wash your hands in the church bathroom before the ceremony starts.

2 ✪ When the time comes to get out of the church pew and walk to the front of the altar, don't talk to your friends or discuss politics on

the phone like you would when waiting for a table at TGI Friday's. This is a holy event so act humble, stay quiet, and start thinking about what you are about to do, which is partake of the body of Christ for Christ's sake! When you get to the altar, kneel down (or remain standing, depending on the parish) and wait for the priest to hand you a communion wafer, also known as the Host.

3 ☯ There are two ways to accept the wafer. Don't grab. You can hold out your hands or open your mouth. If you want the priest to put the wafer in your hands, cradle one hand in the palm of the other and keep your fingers closed. If you want the priest to place the wafer directly in your mouth (which he will do), keep your hands down and open the mouth wide and slightly stick out your tongue when it's your turn.

4 ☯ If you've accepted the wafer by hand, stand up and step to the side so the next person can come forward, and put the wafer in your mouth right then and there. Do not take it back to your seat with you. This is considered disrespectful. Also, don't remove the Host from your mouth, put it in your pocket or toss it under the pew in front of you. The priest and a team of stern-looking nuns will find you, rap you on the knuckles with a wooden ruler, swat your behind with a paddle, ply you with guilt, and who knows what else.

Do-It-Yourself Gluten-Free Communion Wafers

If you like taking communion but you just can't bear to go to church one more time to listen to the old Catholic priest drone on about crucifixion, death, and sin, try holding a Mass at home! All you need to do is go buy a bottle of Ernest and Julio Gallo and a few tiny cups. For the Host, invite some friends over and make it yourself! When it comes time to hand them out, whoever's house you're in gets to be the priest.

You Will Need:

2 tablespoons potato starch
⅞ cup cornstarch
3 cups brown or white rice flour
1 teaspoon baking soda
1 teaspoon salt
2 tablespoons xanthum gum
½ cup margarine
1 cup buttermilk

Steps to Enlightenment

1 ✿ Preheat the oven to 350 degrees.

2 ✿ Mix together the first six ingredients.

3 ✿ Cut in the margarine.

4 ✿ Add buttermilk and mix everything together with your fingers until the dough is thick but malleable.

5 ✿ Then sprinkle the rice flour onto a clean smooth surface and roll out the dough with a rolling pin until it's as thin as possible.

6 ✿ Use bottle caps or the top of a really small jar to cut out circles of dough.

7 ✿ Bake for six minutes, taking care not to overcook the body of Christ. If you do, say ten Hail Marys and start from the top.

8 ✿ Serves several hundred.

Word to the Wise

Keep the wafers in an airtight container until used. You wouldn't want the body of Christ to get stale.

Yoga Dining

In India, yogis—those who practice yoga—have a way of dining that can only be described as awakened eating. Just as yogic exercises release the body's dormant energy sources in order to unite oneself with a higher consciousness, eating can be a way to discover the vital energy and consciousness found in foods, an energy Indians call *rasa*.

In a sense, the *rasa* or prime energy of any living thing is its soul, so with no disrespect to collard greens and smothered chicken, fruits and vegetables eaten by yogic standards could be the real soul food. Imagine being so present and eating a mango so deliberately that you connect with its juicy, sweet essence. You're not only taking dining to a sensual level but you're contributing to the enlightenment of your own soul. After much practice, you'll end up gravitating toward the food that your body and soul really need.

In the same way that practicing yoga exercises requires a focus on breathing and body posture, practicing yoga dining needs a certain mindfulness as you tuck in to the day's dinner.

You Will Need:

Foods that you enjoy eating and that can be eaten with your hands

Steps to Enlightenment

1 ☯ Sit at a table with the food spread out in front of you. Then practice deep abdominal breathing as you would before a yoga exercise, so as to calm and clear the mind.

2 ✿ Slowly begin to focus on the food in front of you. Notice the different shapes and sizes, the colors and textures.

3 ✿ When something you notice looks particularly good, reach out for it and hold it in your hand. Now slowly notice the texture of the food and how heavy, hot, or cold it is.

4 ✿ The next step is to bring the food close to your nose and give it a good smell. Taking in the fresh aroma of a food is the first step to knowing it and connecting with it.

5 ✿ Then bite into the food. First, notice the sound it makes as you chew it and then recognize its flavors during the entire chewing process. Consciously think about what the flavor is according to the six basic flavors: sweet, sour, salty, pungent, bitter, and astringent. Practice this with every bite—yoga dining is a way to train your tastes to recognize each food for exactly what it is.

Word to the Wise

Slowing down and enjoying food in this way helps you truly enjoy eating rather than just stuffing something in as a filler.

Five-Star Enlightenment:
Spiritually Enhancing Fine Dining

Eating for enlightenment isn't limited to communion wafers or a single highly conscious apple. Some of the best times in life are had around white-tableclothed tables set with fine silver and two wineglasses, as a waiter (or two) serves you and your guests the finest food money can buy. Imagine spending $500 on sushi or $800 on foie gras, steak au poivre, and a 1990 vintage Château Mouton Rothschild. Toss in some fine conversation and a perfectly crisp crème brûlé and prepare your soul for liftoff.

The three things a perfect restaurant must have in order for their guests to achieve enlightenment through eating (and in order to get five stars) are good food, good atmosphere, and good service. A place with succulent duck and cool lighting that has a waiter who can't tell you what's in the truffle sauce will only make you feel like you're getting ripped off. Similarly, if someone is asking you to pay $32 for steak tenderloin but the lights are so bright that you can see every freckle on your date's eyelid, then there'll be no enlightened dining there.

What you really want is a restaurant that makes you feel special and, to use industry lingo, "taken care of." The best way to go is to hand the menu back to your waiter after he or she hands it to you and say, "Bring me what the chef recommends." When he or she asks you about wine, you say, "Yes, we'll start with white and then move on to red." Then sit back and let the courses start coming out. A good restaurant (and a good chef) will know what to do to make your evening sing.

Cooking Up Total Enlightenment

When you cook you create, and any time those juices get flowing you're setting yourself up for a soulful experience with food. Of course, this can't happen all the time. Take, for example, the frozen pizza dinner. The only "cooking" involved is you breaking open the box and turning the oven on. Plus there's no way you can know exactly what's gone into that frozen Frisbee and if you could know you probably wouldn't want to. So, the key to enlightened cooking is this: Slow down, use fresh ingredients, and invite friends over who will bring wine and good conversation. Your gift to them is a home-cooked meal.

Lover's Lusty Chocolate Cake

If enlightenment is love, then chocolate is your food of choice. Researchers have determined that when we "fall in love" our brains release mood elevating endorphins and a feel-good chemical known as phenylethylamine—the very same thing that is triggered by eating chocolate. Love potion #9? Could be.

You Will Need:

2½ cups cake flour
1½ teaspoons baking soda
1 teaspoon salt
1½ sticks unsalted butter, at room temperature
2 cups sugar
3½ ounces high quality semisweet dark chocolate, melted
    and cooled
1 teaspoon vanilla extract
2 eggs
1½ cups cold water
Chambord raspberry liqueur, for drizzling
Chocolate cream icing (see recipe on page 133)

Steps to Chocolate Enlightenment

1 ✿ Position an oven rack in the center of the oven and preheat the oven to 350 degrees.

2 ✿ In a large bowl, sift together the flour, baking soda, and salt; set aside. In the bowl of an electric mixer, cream the butter and the sugar until light and fluffy. Add the cooled chocolate and vanilla and beat

for 3 minutes to incorporate. Beat in the eggs one at a time. Scrape down the sides of the bowl and beat for another 3 minutes. Gradually mix in the dry ingredients in 3 batches, alternating with the cold water. Beat for 1 minute after each addition to incorporate the ingredients. Mix until the batter is smooth.

3 ✿ Coat 2 (9-inch) round cake pans with nonstick cooking spray. Cut 2 circles of parchment paper to fit the pan bottoms and place them inside the pans. Pour batter into the prepared pans; they should be ⅔ full. Bake for 30 to 35 minutes, or until a toothpick inserted in the center comes out clean .

4 ✿ Cool for 40 minutes. Turn the cakes out of the pans and remove the paper. Drizzle them with a few tablespoons of Chambord.

5 ✿ Spread ½ cup chocolate icing in middle of one layer and work your way out. Carefully place the second layer on top. Smooth the sides with icing, then spread the rest over the top so that the cake is completely covered. Refrigerate for 5 minutes before decorating or cutting.

Chocolate Cream Icing

You Will Need:

3 cups powdered sugar
7 tablespoons hot water
4 ounces bittersweet dark chocolate, melted and cooled
2 teaspoons vanilla extract
½ stick unsalted butter, at room temperature
¼ cup semisweet dark chocolate, finely chopped

Steps to Chocolate Enlightenment

1 ❧ In the bowl of an electric mixer, dissolve the sugar in water at low speed.

2 ❧ Beat in the dark chocolate and vanilla.

3 ❧ Add butter gradually in small bits and mix until everything is completely incorporated.

4 ❧ Using a spatula, fold in the chopped chocolate and give a final quick spin.

Denise's Homemade Peach Ice Cream

This recipe is one part hot summer day, a front porch, and lots of fans, one part sweat and work from hand-cranking the ice cream maker, and one part pure unadulterated soul-filling goodness. Mix ingredients in a seeker's soul and achieve enlightenment.

You Will Need:

1½ cup peach pulp from best smelling ripe peaches you can find
1½ cup granulated sugar
Juice of 1 lemon
1 qt half and half
A hand-cranked ice cream maker
Rock salt
At least one 2-pound bag of ice

Steps to Enlightenment

1 ❧ Remove the pit, or stone, from the choice, ripe peaches.

2 ✏ Chop them in a food processor to make small chunks of peach. If you don't have a food processor, pare the peaches and rub the pulp through a puree strainer for a fine texture.

3 ✏ Mix the peaches and the rest of the ingredients right inside the can of your ice cream maker, put the lid on, and set it inside the maker.

4 ✏ Pack the maker with ice and rock salt, using three parts crushed ice to one part salt. Crank away until the ice cream is thick.

Father Ted's Chocolate Chip Cookies

Bake sale at church? House warming gift for the new neighbors? Sweet tooth acting up? These chocolate chip cookies will bring you money, friends, and pleasure. What else do you want?

You Will Need:

2 cups plus 2 tablespoons all purpose flour
½ teaspoon baking soda
½ teaspoon salt
¾ cup unsalted butter
1 cup dark brown sugar, firmly packed
½ cup granulated sugar
2 large eggs
2 teaspoons pure vanilla extract
2 cups semisweet chocolate chips

Steps to Enlightenment

1 ✏ Melt the butter in a saucepan, then let it begin to cool.

2 ✿ Adjust your oven racks so that one is in the upper position and the other is just below the middle. Then preheat the oven to 325 degrees.

3 ✿ Sift flour with baking soda and salt. Set aside.

4 ✿ Cream the butter and sugars thoroughly in a mixer.

5 ✿ Beat in one egg and add only the yolk of a second one. Then beat in the vanilla until combined.

6 ✿ Add the dry ingredients and beat everything at low speed just until combined.

7 ✿ Add the chocolate chips.

8 ✿ Roll a scant ¼ cup of dough into a ball. Gently pull it into two halves. Press the sides of the two halves together so that the rough edges face up.

9 ✿ Leave 2½ inches between each dough ball on cookie sheet and bake.

10 ✿ After 8 minutes, reverse position of cookie sheets. Bake an additional 7 to 10 minutes or until cookies are lightly golden brown and edges are starting to harden but centers are soft and puffy.

11 ✿ Eat one right out of the oven with a glass of whole milk and ascend to heaven.

Fasting and Cleansing

"The best of all medicines are rest and fasting."

—Benjamin Franklin

There's no question that eating duck foie gras, Swiss chocolate, and homemade peach ice cream will send you to the moon. But try not eating anything at all . . . for several days. One thing's certain; If you have been stuffing in all kinds of rich foods and then you stop, you're going to crash, and hard. Still, for most of us, not eating, or eating only liquids like juice or water for several days at a stretch—a process known as fasting—is yet another way to achieve enlightenment.

Historically, fasting has been practiced by Hindus, Buddhists, Muslims, Catholics, Native Americans, and high-school girls for centuries. Mostly, religious or spiritual fasting is a ritual surrounding a special time of year such as Lent, Ramadan, or the Senior Prom. It is usually preceded by extensive gorging and partying (e.g., Mardi Gras).

Medically speaking, fasting can be a way to cleanse your body— specifically the intestinal tract, including the colon—of stored toxins, parasites, and heavy metals. When combined with saunas, meditation, and (gasp!) enemas, things really start to get enlightening.

Basically, there are enzymes inside your body that help break down food. When there is no food to break down, those same enzymes start breaking down damaged cells, unwelcome microbes, metabolic wastes, and pollutants. Fasting also gives your body's organs a rest. Instead of wrestling all night with the steak tartare you had the day before, they can conserve energy and work more toward eliminating the bad stuff you collect. There are several different kinds of fasts you can do, but a three-day juice fast is the recommended one for first-timers. When you're done with that, try a coffee enema. Yippee!

The Juice Fast

Juicing and drinking vegetables and fruits is preferable for many folks to just cutting out food altogether. It's also a little more healthy than just cutting out eating altogether and going on a hunger strike (which by the way is a great fast to do if you happen to be a political prisoner or activist trying to get your message across). With the juice fast, you get good vitamins and minerals without eating solids. Also, the fibrous nature of fruits and vegetables will get things loosened up in no time. And oh boy, if you've been struggling with constipation, this is about as enlightening as it gets.

You Will Need:

As many different organic fresh vegetables as you can get your
    hands on
A small amount of organic fresh fruit
Filtered water
A juicer
Three days
A bathroom
Plenty of toilet paper

Steps to Enlightenment

1 ✺ On the first day, squeeze yourself eight ounces of fruit juice for breakfast and then whenever you feel hungry or thirsty during the rest of the day, make yourself an eight-ounce glass of vegetable juice to consume. Make sure that each glass is 25 percent water.

2 ✺ On the second day, start cutting out fruit juices, as they have a high sugar content and will make you "feel" hungry. As on the first

day, drink a vegetable juice whenever you feel hungry or thirsty, but do not drink more than six glasses of juice.

3 ✿ On the third day, limit your juice consumption to four eight-ounce glasses.

4 ✿ When it's time to break the fast, it's important not to dive into a Philly Cheese Steak right away. Ease back into eating solid foods by consuming light foods like fruit, raw vegetables, and cottage cheese. Also, don't stuff yourself. Meals should be small but frequent.

Word to the Wise

The second day will be the hardest, as the toxins in your body begin to make themselves known through things such as bad breath and possibly headaches. Try to take your mind off eating by going for walks (not too strenuous and not too far from a bathroom!), reading spiritual texts, or hanging out with friends. Enlightenment will come mid-morning on the third day as you start to imagine yourself levitating over a vat of chocolate pudding.

The Coffee Enema

Any time you introduce a stream of liquid into your rectum you can't help but achieve some kind of enlightenment. And believe it or not, putting coffee in your enema bag is not some kind of underground rave trip. It actually helps detoxify your liver, which in turn helps get rid of additional harmful toxins in the rest of your body.

You Will Need:

Large saucepan
Organic ground coffee (skip the Folger's)

Filtered water
An enema bag
KY Jelly or some kind of lubricant

Steps to Enlightenment

1 ✿ Boil about a quart of filtered water in a saucepan and add two tablespoons of ground coffee.

2 ✿ Let it boil for at least another three minutes to ensure that any impurities in the coffee or water are killed.

3 ✿ Let the mixture cool down to a *very comfortable* temperature. Needless to say, don't pump steaming hot liquid into your butt. You don't want it cold, either.

4 ✿ Pour the coffee mixture in the enema bag and let some of the liquid run out of the tube before clamping it shut. This removes any air.

5 ✿ Lie down in a comfortable place where you can hang the bag on a door knob or similarly high spot. Be sure and put some old towels under you because there's going to be coffee everywhere.

6 ✿ Lube up the end of the enema tube and insert it about two inches into your rectum. Release the clamp and let about two cups of coffee flow gently into your rectum (too hard and the coffee might go too high into the colon, which will put caffeine in the bloodstream— another form of enlightenment, but not the one we're going for here).

7 ✿ Clamp the tube if you feel any kind of discomfort. Hold the coffee in for at least ten minutes before letting it go over the toilet bowl.

8 ✿ Repeat these steps one more time for a total of two enemas and feel the power!

The Perfect Passover

Passover, or Pesach in Hebrew, is an important Jewish holiday and feast commemorating the passage in Exodus when the Angel of Death "passed over" Jewish and Egyptian homes in Egypt around 1300 BCE. Jews whose doors were marked with the blood of a ritual sacrifice were saved, while those Egyptians who did not mark their doors with blood (i.e., all of them) had their firstborn male children killed. Pretty harsh, no? But the Jewish people gained their freedom from their Egyptian captors, eventually leading to lots of wandering in the wilderness and a reunion with the Promised Land.

Now the event is celebrated in the spring, on the first full moon after the vernal equinox. For most Jews, the large feast, known as the seder, occurs on the first day of Passover, and it celebrates the Jewish exodus from Egypt. Six different foods are placed on a seder plate including *karpas* (vegetables dipped in salt water), *maror* (bitter herbs), *chazeret* (bitter vegetables), *charoset* (apple, nuts, and spices with wine), *zeroa* (lamb shankbone) and *beitzah* (roasted egg). Each item holds a symbolic meaning and all but the last two are eaten in the order they appear here (the last two are purely symbolic and are not to be eaten). Also, there are a variety of ritual readings from the Haggadah along with oral explanations of the food during the meal. These are sparked by questions that the children in the room are encouraged to ask, such as "Grandpa, why are we eating such nasty stuff?"

Ironically, enlightenment doesn't come easy with these ancient religious traditions, but that doesn't mean you can't get it. You just have to shake things up a bit. Spruce up the atmosphere, break out some wine, and treat the seder like you would any other dinner party with friends. After all, this feast is all about celebrating freedom!

Cooking the Passover Seder

All of the food served at your Passover seder party doesn't all have to be of the bitter, salty variety (though a few of those will be included on the seder plate). While many traditional dinners surrounding the ritual food consist of veal stew, unleavened bread, matzo balls, and gefilte fish loaves, yours can be more, shall we say, tasty. If gefilte fish makes you a cold fish, skip it. Try rockfish covered with lobster sauce or lamb in a blood orange juice and red wine sauce instead. The only thing that really matters is the seder plate.

You Will Need:

Potatoes, onions, and radishes (for the *karpas*)

Romaine lettuce and dried horseradish (for the *chazeret* and *maror*)

Water

Salt

Apples, walnuts, almonds, cinnamon, and ginger (for the *charoset*)

Red wine (for the *charoset* and the chef)

A lamb shank bone (for the *zeroa*)

One egg, roasted (for the *beitzah*)

Steps to Enlightenment

Chazeret and *Karpas*

1 ✿ Boil the potatoes until soft.

2 ✿ Slice onions and radishes into bite-sized pieces.

3 ✿ Use a raw piece of romaine lettuce for the *chazeret*.

4 ✿ Place the *chazeret* on the plate. The salt water should go on the table next to the seder plate.

5 ✿ These bitter vegetables make up two dishes—one with salt water (the *karpas*) and one without. Both symbolize the bitterness of slavery.

Maror

1 ✿ Place a large leaf of romaine lettuce on the seder plate.

2 ✿ Grate the dried horseradish and place it alongside the lettuce.

3 ✿ Like the *karpas* and *chazeret* dishes, this dish of "bitter herbs" recalls the embittered lives Jewish slaves led under the Egyptians.

Charoset

1 ✿ This dish is supposed to remind the Jewish people of the mortar and bricks lugged around by Hebrew slaves. It doesn't sound like it's going to taste good, but it's the best of the bunch.

2 ✿ Chop the nuts, apples, and ginger into coarse bits. Mix in cinnamon and only enough wine to make everything moist (about two tablespoons).

Zeroa

1 ✿ Some people use a lamb shankbone, broiled to cook the meat left on it. Others use a broiled chicken neck. Either one represents the Passover sacrifice made in the ancient temple. You probably wouldn't have anyway, but don't eat this dish. It's only part of the ritual.

Beitzah

1 ✿ Hard boil one egg and then partially broil it to a golden brown. This symbolizes mourning, sacrifice, spring, and renewal. It is not to be eaten.

Word to the Wise

The food on the seder plate should go in the following order, moving around the plate clockwise: *chazeret* (lettuce), *karpas* (vegetable), *beitzah*

(roasted egg), *zeroa* (roasted bone), and *charoset* (nuts and apples). The *maror* (bitter herbs) goes in the center.

How to Be the Perfect Passover Host

Think back to seders of old, when you were a child and your great-grandmother would come over with smelly cold gefilte fish and day-old matzo balls. Try to remember all the things that made you want to run away and become a Christian, such as when your Uncle Ben always wanted to argue about the Palestinian conflict or your Aunt Edith tried to tell you that life was a bitch. These are things you don't want to repeat when you host your own Passover seder.

Instead, get some friends to come over with wine and good music. Host the party like you would any other—with planning and energy. You might want to spend some time cooking and cleaning the house before everyone gets there, but if some food isn't ready, pour some wine and start asking friends to do specific tasks like dishing up the *charoset* or broiling the *beitzah*.

If you know you're having non-Jews come over, consider printing out a page of the reasons behind the meal and put together a step-by-step guide of how things are eaten and what's read beforehand. For everyone's sake, it might also be helpful to print out a list of questions for some to ask and a list of responses for others to announce. This is a little like putting on a play, so have fun with it.

Also, don't forget basic hosting, such as making sure everyone is having a good time. If you see someone sitting or standing alone, it's polite to go talk to them or try to draw them into conversation with someone else (and then tactfully leave). Discourage too much wine drinking before eating by serving the food sooner rather than later. Even if you have a few drunk Passover guests, the bitter *maror* will bring them around like a fistful of smelling salts.

Ten Fun Passover Party Tips

For a truly enlightening time, throw in a few of these tips and watch the yarmulkes fly!

1 ✿ If the seder is getting a little stale, bring in some live music. It doesn't have to be traditional, but that would work as well. *The Ten Plagues* is a common Jewish rock band name.

2 ✿ Invite your worrying Jewish aunt over for thirty minutes (and thirty minutes only). Have her talk to as many people as possible about why Passover is such a big deal. That ought to give everyone something fresh to talk about.

3 ✿ Pretend to eat the roasted *beitzah* by putting food coloring on a hard-boiled egg (to make it look like it's been broiled) and then popping it in your mouth. Wait to see the dismay on everyone's face before producing the real *beitzah* (which you carefully hid behind your back).

4 ✿ Secretly allow the dog to jump up and grab the *zeroa*, then watch as the entire congregation chases the beast around the room trying to wrest control of the sacrificial bone.

5 ✿ Place a whoopie cushion on your neighbor's seat as he or she gets up to reach for a matzo ball.

6 ✿ Serve a plate of regular leavened bread instead of unleavened bread and wait to see if anyone notices.

7 ✿ Put your little brother up to asking, "Where did I come from?" instead of "Why isn't the bread fluffy?"

8 ✿ Pretend to sneeze or cough out a piece of *charoset*.

9 ✿ Provide fake gray beards and mustaches for your guests so you can all pretend to be rabbis.

10 ✿ Sew propellers to a few yarmulkes as party gifts.

The thing to do when working on a motorcycle, as in any other task, is to cultivate the peace of mind, which does not separate one's self from one's surroundings. When that is done successfully then everything else follows naturally. Peace of mind produces right values, right values produce right thoughts. Right thoughts produce right actions and right actions produce work which will be a material reflection for others to see of the serenity at the center of it all.

—ROBERT PIRSIG, *Zen and the Art of Motorcycle Maintenance*

c h a p t e r
FIVE

Enlightenment Through Work

Enlightenment through work may sound like an oxymoron to most, but look at it this way: Most of us have to work, so why not find some spirit in it? Whether you're digging ditches, trading stocks, or dishing out soup to those less fortunate, work is how we participate in life. For some, that means giving back what we've learned and earned. For others, it's a way to pass the day with some purpose. Both are a way to gain a sense of accomplishment, which grounds a person, gives them self-worth, nurtures confidence, and allows them to sock money away for a pilgrimage to the Himalayas, where you can't swing a dead yak without knocking into a higher power. So whether it's a means to an end or an end in itself (as Camus's Sisyphus would argue), work breeds enlightenment. You just have to know where to look for it.

Enlightenment Through Manual Labor

Blood, sweat, and curse words can only come from those who work hard—and I'm talking about the kind of work that entails lifting, digging, hauling, and anything that doesn't involve too much responsibility. This is what's known around construction sites as manual labor. Though not a lot of thought is required for jobs like these, that doesn't mean that manual laborers are dumb. In fact, they may be the smartest of us all. Here is work that is simple, easy to learn, and free of office politics of all kinds. Like focusing on a candle flame during meditation or on a chakra point during yoga, setting out to dig a four-foot-long and three-foot-deep ditch can clear the mind, focus your energy, and make you centered. Plus, at the end of the day, there is true satisfaction from seeing exactly what you've accomplished—a point not lost on an increasingly more global economy.

Techniques for Digging

Digging holes, whether you're planting trees or laying a foundation, is a great way to clear the mind and get in touch with yourself—two essential steps for finding total enlightenment. Just make sure you get the right shovel for the job you're doing and don't chop off a toe or get carpal tunnel syndrome in the process. Those things tend to muddle the mind and make you literally lose touch with yourself (as the tips of your toes end up in the dirt).

You Will Need:

A shovel
Steel-tipped work boots with metal shanks
The willingness to sweat
Dirt

Steps to Enlightenment

1 ✿ Mentally determine the parameters of the hole you plan to dig. Then mark the area with your shovel by either scraping a line in the

dirt or by cutting into the soil with the tip of your shovel along the perimeter.

2 ↺ Starting at the center of the hole, place the tip of your shovel in the ground so that the spade is at an angle and the handle of the shovel is perpendicular to the ground.

3 ↺ To sink the blade in the ground, use one foot to step on one of the kick plates on top of the spade. Try not to jump on the shovel with two feet as you might risk a) having the shovel handle whack you in the chest and b) looking silly.

4 ↺ When the blade is in the ground, bend your knees, place one hand on the end of the shovel handle and one hand close to the spade and lift with your shoulders. Make sure your back is straight and focus on using your shoulders and legs—not your back—to lift the dirt out of the hole.

5 ↺ Pitch the dirt off to one side and repeat steps 3 and 4, working in rhythm.

Word to the Wise

Eventually your body movement will become so natural that your mind will be able to wander from the task at hand. Let it. As the movement begins to increase heart rate and blood flow, forcing sweat and toxins out of your pores, allow any thoughts or worries to well up in your mind. Let yourself ponder them for a while before letting them go. Just as you are digging dirt out of the hole, imagine that you are digging up thoughts and stresses and tossing them aside. Soon your mind will clear. If no thoughts come, focus on the sound of the shovel going in the dirt. Listen for birds and the sounds of nature. Let yourself become connected to the earth and allow yourself to notice your body digging in the dirt. Eventually, digging will introduce you to a simple meditative state of being.

Gardening Basics

Ever notice that people who garden seem to be calm and rosy cheeked? That's because all that time spent in the sun, digging in the dirt, and nurturing seeds to maturity and plants to good health has taught them the ancient wisdom of Mother Earth or Gaia. It's a wisdom that links all living things together through nature. Cultivating the land to grow healthy plants is essentially the same thing as cultivating good health for yourself and your neighbors, thereby making body and soul robust and vibrant.

You Will Need:

A small spade
A handheld spade fork
Hand clippers
Long-handled pruning clippers
Round point shovel
Wheelbarrow
Watering can
Hose and/or soaker hose
Gardening gloves
A large-brimmed hat
Packets of vegetable and flower seeds
A few small patches of Mother Earth

Steps to Enlightenment

1 ✿ Before you plant anything in the ground, be sure and test the acid content or the pH balance of your soil. Either that or ask a local nursery about the soil in your area—most will know soil conditions in your town. Depending on where you live, you might have to add fertilizers,

composts, or plain old topsoil to enrich the existing soil and even out the pH. Simply turn these added materials into your existing soil with a shovel.

2 ☙ Generally, the best time to plant new flowers, ground covers, or shrubs is in April after the last freeze has come and gone.

3 ☙ Flowers are a form of enlightenment all on their own, especially when they're blooming and brightening up your house. There are two categories of flowers you can plant: perennials and annuals. Perennials such as roses and bulbs are hardy flowers that live for many years and bloom for a few weeks every year at the same time. Annuals grow, bloom, and die for only one year, but they can bloom for months.

4 ☙ Seed packets will explain what kinds of conditions a particular flower will want, whether that's shade, sun, partial shade, lots of water, or none at all. Plant accordingly.

5 ☙ If you want to plant a vegetable garden, dig up a rectangular patch of ground that will stay in full sunlight most of the year.

6 ☙ Vegetable seeds grow best on raised rows so that they don't sit in pools of water. Make sure these rows run from east to west so everything gets the right amount of sun.

7 ☙ When you plant, sprinkle seeds along the length of each row and press them about a ½ inch into the soil with your finger. Then water each row as soon as possible. It's also fun to label your crops so you don't forget what you planted when all these green, tall plants start to shoot up out of the ground.

8 ☙ New flowers, plants, and trees need a lot of watering when they first go into the ground in spring. In the summer months, it's best to water in the early morning and at dusk when it's not so hot outside.

Word to the Wise

Planting flowers and vegetables is only the first step in keeping healthy plants strong. Water on a regular basis and spend ten or fifteen minutes a day keeping the weeds away. Make no mistake, the work of nurturing your plants is also the work of nurturing your soul.

Enlightenment Through Making Lots of Money

Money has been called the root of all evil, but usually by those who don't have any of it. There's no doubt that collecting greenbacks—and lots of them—can be truly enlightening if that's what you want to do. Just look at Bill Gates. He has made so much dough that instead of spending time worrying about how to pay the rent (time, mind you, that we could all use to help focus our minds on more enlightening pursuits), he spends time giving money to help poor children in India get better healthcare. The short of it is that being smart, wise, and hardworking doesn't mean you have to be poor and that if you have the opportunity to make money it doesn't mean you have to be a soulless Grinch when your bank account starts to swell.

Ways to Get Rich (and Find Enlightenment) Quick

1 ☻ Head to Vegas. With lady luck on your side, and your kids' college fund, you can double your money in no time. (Disclaimer: Gambling isn't particularly enlightening if you lose.)

2 ☻ Play the lottery. Some might say you have a better chance of getting hit by a meteorite than hitting the Mega-Millions lottery jackpot, but hey, you'll never know until you play.

3 ✿ Become a day trader and play the stock market. This one's a little like going to Vegas but at least it has a professional tone to it.

4 ✿ Write books (just kidding).

5 ✿ Develop a software program that helps people get rich quick.

6 ✿ Buy crates of water filters and sell them door-to-door as part of a pyramid scheme. Oh wait, pyramid schemes never work unless you invent your own and get other people to play along.

7 ✿ Invent a pyramid scheme.

8 ✿ Sell your body to science. Folks get paid all the time for donating blood and plasma and for agreeing to test out new drugs. The only drawback with this is if you take a drug that turns you into a vegetable who can only stay alive by artificial means. There will be no enlightenment forthcoming in those situations.

9 ✿ Discover and produce the next boy band.

10 ✿ Get a large corporation to sponsor your path to enlightenment and then spend the money lavishly as a means to total enlightenment.

Volunteering: Working for Others Less Fortunate

Helping others who can't help themselves earns big karma points. Plus, when you give your time and energy to those who need it, especially children, you're able to inspire others with your kindness and goodwill. And that achieves enlightenment for you and those you inspire!

Where you choose to volunteer can also help you along your personal vision quest. You can clean animal shelters, offer support for iron man and marathon races, help out at film or music festivals, sign up to help build backcountry paths in national parks—the list can be as long as your imagination (after all, who's going to turn down a chance to have someone work for free).

For those who want to travel, there are numerous groups that would gladly take you on as long as you pay your airfare and expenses in the country you're visiting. Even if you don't want to leave your hometown or even your house, you can volunteer online to help tutor and mentor kids as well as a hundred other possibilities.

Here are two groups that can help you find local volunteer opportunities in your area:

Youth Service America's ServeNet—www.servenet.org/
Volunteer Match—www.volunteermatch.org/

For those wanting to travel and volunteer, check out:

Global Volunteers—www.globalvolunteers.org/
The American Hiking Society—www.americanhiking.org/
Cross-Cultural Solutions—www.crossculturalsolutions.org/
Earthwatch Institute—www.earthwatch.org/
Habitat for Humanity International—www.habitat.org/
Volunteers for Peace—www.vfp.org/
The Sierra Club—http://www.sierraclub.org/

Home Work: Basic Cleaning Techniques

Unless you've found enlightenment through making lots of money, cleaning house is probably something you have to do. If you don't do it and your place is filthy, you probably don't get to experience too many enlightening dates (see Chapter 7). Either way, cleaning can inspire and it can humble, which peels away inflated egos to reveal the true self within. Purging your house of clutter is also the first step toward a calm, material-free existence, which, according to the Buddhists, is a way to do away with distraction, focus the mind, and suffer less in life (material possessions only breed suffering because they promote desire).

Steps to Enlightenment

1 ✪ Start a routine. Each day do something to help keep the house orderly and clean, such as making your bed and doing the dishes after you use them. On the same day every week, do the big stuff like cleaning the bathroom and sweeping and mopping the floor (which by the way won't take as long as it would if you do it once a month).

2 ✪ If the path you're on starts to get too busy with frequent pilgrimages, daily meditations, shrine building consultation and the like, and the work of cleaning the house starts to overwhelm you, then take one room at a time and remind yourself that by doing this job you are doing the daily small things it takes to build a path to enlightenment.

3 ✪ Another way to avoid becoming overwhelmed is to write yourself to-do lists. Between item number 1, "pray to Allah," and item number 10, "make Sunday's communion bread," squeeze in "clean the toilet." By taking on these all-too-human chores, you're actually doing two things: reminding yourself of your mortality (and therefore the fact that you will die some day—an enlightening prospect [see Chapter 2, Part 3: Soul]) and preventing yourself from acquiring a God complex.

4 ✪ In order to achieve simple material-free living (and a cleaner house), try the simple task of putting things away immediately after you use them.

Word to the Wise

Like digging a ditch, sweeping and mopping the floor can be just as enlightening as surfing the big waves on the Big Island's north shore. It's humbling (stripping one of a potentially harmful ego) and since it's repetitive and not too complicated you're able to clear and calm the mind while taking pleasure in walking barefoot through your house without raisins or spilled coffee sticking to your feet.

Jesus Was a Carpenter: Basic Carpentry

Whether or not Jesus really was a carpenter is up for interpretation. Some say he was, which showed his down-to-earth, everyman side. Others say it was just a symbolic title given to a man who used the "tools" given to him to "construct" an uplifting message. Still others say Jesus wasn't a real man at all and that he was a made-up story based on the many archetypal figures that have been passed down through hundreds of civilizations and spiritual belief systems for thousands of years (Krishna and Prometheus both have enormous similarities to Jesus). But that's a different discussion.

Building something with your hands and a few tools (power or otherwise) can leave a strong feeling of fulfillment and worth. If you work behind a computer most days, building offers a great physical balance to your otherwise cerebral existence. And as we found out in Chapter 2, balance equals enlightenment.

Carpentry and building also has the ability to root you in one of the most primal human instincts: the need to build shelter. Not all of us are going to build houses, but even if you construct a children's toy box out of wood, you'll get the feeling that you could throw up a few walls and a roof if you had to. And that could come in handy should you ever find yourself wandering in the wilderness for a couple of years.

Carpentry: Basic Tool List

Clawhammer with a fiberglass shaft

3.5 amp variable-speed, corded or cordless electric drill

7¼-inch circular power saw

25-foot steel tape measure

2-foot level

Torpedo level

Hacksaw

Set of chisels

Set of Phillips head and flathead screwdrivers

Slip-joint pliers

Needle-nose pliers

Drill bit set

Nail punch

Utility knife with razors

Wood plane

A toolbox to house all of the above

Carpentry Techniques

The rules of carpentry are simple, really: Measure accurately and cut straight. In fact, an old carpenter friend used to tell me that it doesn't matter how many times you measure, only how many times you cut the wood. In other words, take the time to measure and be sure about the length, down to a sixteenth of an inch, before you make your cut.

The other cardinal rule is to make things level and plumb (i.e., square). Building things out of square has a domino effect: One corner out of square skews all others.

There are lots of other tricks of the trade, most of which can be found in any number of do-it-yourself manuals and building guides. They're a good place to start. That said, you won't feel confident about building until you dive into a project. The more experience and practice you get, the better you'll become.

Lastly, water is the great enemy of wood, so if you're building outside with wood, make sure you've planned for water getting on it. Seal it, flash around edges and think ahead so that you won't be leaving any wood standing in pools of water. Wood is like a sponge and it will soak up water just like a sponge, which then promotes wood rot, insects, and more time and money spent fixing those things.

Building Project

A handyman's enlightenment doesn't come with tools and knowledge alone. You have to put what you know (and your power tools) to work and gain some real experience. While you're at it, you might as well build something that will help you along the path to enlightenment.

Open-Aired Japanese Teahouse and Meditation Platform

Japanese carpentry has a long and distinguished history based around temple building for the Shinto and Buddhist religions. Because both of these spiritual paths hold nature in high regard (both originally worshiped outside), the use of wood in their temples was essential for its symbolism and its physical properties. Japanese carpenters revered wood because they believed that it remained a living organism even after it was cut. Great care was given and specific methods were used when a tree was cut down to ensure that the boards harvested from the trunk would continue on as a living thing of beauty.

Early temples were also built without using nails, screws, or fasteners of any kind. Instead, carpenters crafted the wood into complex joints that could withstand typhoons, earthquakes, and heavy roof loads.

Temples were always built in the post-and-beam style, which means the corner posts were buried in the ground and the floor, walls, and ceiling were hung off these poles.

This teahouse and meditation platform is built in the post-and-beam style, but don't worry about harvesting your own tree, though if you did it would most certainly offer further enlightenment. And go ahead and use nails. Learning traditional Japanese carpentry takes about twenty-five years to perfect.

You Will Need:

4 10-foot 4 x 4 posts (all wood is cedar)
2 6-foot 2 x 6—the floor beams
4 10-foot 2 x 4—the floor joists
7 6-foot 1 x 6—the roof rafters and side rims of roof
1 8-foot 1 x 6—the roof ridge
2 6-foot 1 x 3—trim for the roof

24 6-foot 1 x 6—floor decking

8 x 10 piece of canvas for roof

Bamboo shades or beads for sides

Posthole digger

Shovel

4 80-pound bags ready-mix cement

8 7-inch galvanized lag bolts with nuts

16 6-inch galvanized lag bolts with nuts

4 metal joist brackets

Box 2 ½-inch 16d galvanized deck screws

About 24 wooden stakes (short and tall)

Mason's string

Hammer

Socket wrench

Steps to Enlightenment

1 ❂ Determine where you want the teahouse to go by driving stakes at about the spots you want the corners to be. To align the corners exactly, set up batter boards (which are two stakes in the ground with a third stake nailed perpendicularly between them) and tie string to them. The batter boards should be set about 3 feet outside each corner. Tie mason's string between the batter boards. Your true corner will be where the strings meet. You might have to adjust the strings along the batter boards to make sure the corners are square. Do this by measuring and comparing the diagonal lengths. A true square will have equal diagonals.

2 ❂ Dig the post holes to a depth of 2 feet. It might be necessary to remove the string at this point. If you do, mark the location of the string on the batter boards with a nail or pencil mark. You want to dig

just inside each corner so that the outside corner of the 4 x 4 posts will fit squarely into the corner made by the string.

3 ✿ Set the posts in the holes in the ground, making sure to align them with the mason's string. Then mix and pour one bag of cement around each post. If the hole isn't filled up all the way, backfill it with dirt once the concrete dries. Let the cement set up and harden overnight.

4 ✿ Next, attach the 2 x 6 beams to the posts. You want one 2 x 6 to run across the front of the teahouse and one to run across the back. Drill two holes through each end of each 2 x 6 so that they are not one above the other but at a slight angle to each other. Drill corresponding holes into the 4 x 4 posts about 12 inches off the ground. Attach the 2 x 6s using the 7-inch lag bolts, washers, and nuts. Hand tighten the bolts down using a ratchet wrench.

5 ✿ The next step is to put on the 10-foot 2 x 4 floor joists. These are 10 feet long so that you'll have aesthetically pleasing 2-foot overhangs on the front and back of the teahouse. The four joists will be spaced 2 feet apart on center. The first joist will run front to back right on top of the 1 x 6 beam and snug against two 4 x 4 posts. Drill holes through the ends of the board and into corresponding holes in the 4 x 4s and attach using the 6-inch lag bolts. Repeat this step for the joist on the other side of the teahouse. The two middle joists will be secured to the 2 x 6 beams using metal joist brackets or hurricane straps.

6 ✿ Once the floor joists are down, line up and attach the decking by screwing the boards to the joists using two screws for each joist (for a total of eight screws in each decking board). Space each board ⅛ inch apart.

7 ✪ Next, construct the roof. There are two gable ends to the roof. Each end consists of two 6-foot 1 x 6 rafters that meet on either side of an 8-foot long 1 x 6 roof ridge. In order for the rafters to lie flush with the roof ridge, you'll have to cut the ends at 45-degree angles. Then nail each rafter into the roof ridge. Be sure to space each gable end accurately so that the rafters can be attached on the outside edge of the front and back sets of 4 x 4 posts.

8 ✪ When this part of the roof is done, have a friend help and lift the roof into place so that the rafters lie flush with a top portion of the outside faces of the front and back 4 x 4s. Using a pencil, mark the rafters where the bolt holes will go (be sure and stagger the holes, as with the floor beams and joists). Lower the roof to drill the holes. Hold it back in place again and mark the corresponding holes on the 4 x 4s. Lower the roof and drill the holes in the 4 x 4s before attaching the roof permanently in place.

9 ✪ Finish the gable ends by screwing 1 x 3s across the front and back of the teahouse directly to the 4 x 4s. This will create triangle-shaped gable ends for the roof. Also, screw in the roof rim boards to the 4 x 4s on the sides of the teahouse between each gable end.

10 ✪ Drape canvas over the roof ridge and secure it to one roof rim board before pulling it tight on the other side and attaching it there.

11 ✪ Finish out your Japanese teahouse by hanging bamboo beads or shades on the sides and back and hanging candle lanterns off the roof ridge. You might even consider setting up a small shrine to Buddha in one corner so he can watch over and bless your new sacred space.

Word to the Wise

For Asian details and ornamental flourishes, it's possible to bevel and miter the ends of the roof ridge and floor joists. Also, in order to keep the cedar wood's rich reddish brown color, brush on a coat or two of water-proofing sealant.

It ain't home t' ye, though it be the palace of a king,
Until somehow yer soul is sort o' wrapped round everything.

—EDGAR A. GUEST, *A Heap o' Livin'*

SIX

Home and Zen Garden

The places we live in may be where we rest and feed our bodies, but they are also spaces in which our souls can dwell. Rather than coming home from work and stuffing in a frozen enchilada dinner before hitting the pillow, treat your space like a retreat where you can find solace from the crazy world. Simple rooms bathed in sunlight can make meditation easier. The Chinese home philosophy of feng shui can promote happiness and prosperity. Rock gardens and calming water fountains help calm tense shoulders. Put them all together and what you have is a home that facilitates spiritual enlightenment.

Of course, if the house and garden is cluttered and messy with stacks of old junk and invasive weeds, then your space becomes a liability rather than an asset on your quest for peace and enlightenment. But with a little organization, some cultivation, and a few storage additions, you can turn that around. What you want is a home and garden that will regenerate your body, mind, and soul rather than drain them.

The Basics of Feng Shui
(Including How to Pronounce Feng Shui)

We've all heard of feng shui, the Chinese philosophy of arranging your house to improve your personal energy, but pronouncing it is a different story. Lest you appear silly in front of your guests when they comment on how serene and vibrant your newly remodeled house is, feng shui is pronounced "fung shway."

Now that we've cleared that up, let's focus on what it is and how to get it. Feng shui has been around for three thousand years and has to do with how one arranges a person's inner chi, or energy. Just as Chinese medicine promotes a balanced chi by increasing or decreasing energy flows within the body through things like acupuncture, exercise, and healthy eating (see Chapter 2, Part 2: Body), feng shui promotes balanced inner chi in your house by specifying colors, room arrangements, and furniture placement. That way you know where to put the laughing Buddha shrine and the foosball table for full spiritual benefit. The idea is that if one area of your life is sagging (such as your love life, your finances, or your rear end), then the particular energy that's needed to firm it up might be getting blocked because of your interior design. In other words, it may actually be time to take down all those black light posters.

Also, clutter is said to block chi, so just by keeping things clean and simple, you can free up some personal energy (see Simplify Your Life: Get Rid of Clutter, page 168). Then again, wholesale changes like re-painting your interior walls and moving your bedroom to the other side of the house are common feng shui practices. Some people even hire feng shui consultants to work with an architect when designing a new house.

The feng shui floor plan or blueprint is what's known as the *bagua* (pronounced "BAG-wa"). It's a large square (traditionally it's an octa-

gon) that is separated into nine smaller squares that are labeled with general areas of concern in a person's life. These areas are then assigned a color and in some cases an element such as water, air, earth, or fire. Health is always in the middle of the square or octagon and it is surrounded by spiritual self-understanding, family, wealth and prosperity, fame and reputation, relationships, creativity and children (fertility), helpful friends, and travel and career. The corresponding colors are yellow and brown (for health), blue and green, green, purple, red, pink and white, white, gray, and black. The water element aligns with career, wood with family, fire with fame and reputation, metal with creativity and children, and earth with health. You can make a floor plan of your actual house and then lay the *bagua* over it to see what rooms correspond to what.

Once you see the area of the house that corresponds to an area of your life then you can tinker with it to get things just right. For example, let's take the area of the house dealing with spiritual enlightenment (or self-understanding). If you find that no matter what you try you can't achieve enlightenment—not even by eating a giant chocolate bar—then the corresponding area of your house may be stacked full with musty old newspapers or the windows may be dirty and there may not be enough light getting in. A dead house plant may even be un-balancing the energy in that area of the house. All of these things can be remedied with some sprucing up and by adding in some blue and green color either in the form of paint, rugs, curtains, or furniture.

Also try lighting some candles and incense—anything that's going to make the place (and your soul) feel alive.

Word to the Wise

Spending loads of cash at a home improvement store may help with soul improvement, but only if you know how to use the stuff you've bought. A botched paint job that ends in spattered windows and floor with the occasional uneven lines of paint on the ceiling tends to create stress rather than calm. The same goes for if you try to move heavy furniture and throw out your back. Enlightenment is much harder to come by whilst in traction.

Simplify Your Life: Get Rid of Clutter

The second of Buddhism's Four Noble Truths is that the origin of suffering is desire. Essentially that means, the more stuff you have the more miserable you are (desiring possessions will only breed suffering). So it stands to reason that the first step on the path to pain-free living (and total enlightenment) is getting rid of all unnecessary stuff. Not only do you not need to keep all the wrapping paper off every present you've ever received, but owning an Itty-Bitty book lamp, a golf ball–shaped clock, or a personalized back scratcher is tantamount to torture. Chuck it! Here are some tips for clearing out your place and getting down to basic, simple, soulful living.

You Will Need:

A place to put everything
Some good housecleaning music such as *The Bee Gees' Greatest Hits*
A trash bag

Steps to Enlightenment

1 ✿ The first step to a clutter-free space is putting on some good music and going through every room in your house and pulling out anything you don't need or haven't used or worn in the past year. Then take it all to the local Salvation Army or to the dump or sell it in a garage sale and buy some new, less cluttery stuff. This is going to take a certain amount of guts. Tears will be shed. Arguments will happen. But be brave. Think of it as though you are lightening your soul and giving it more room to breathe.

2 ✿ Any clutter that's left should go in a specific place. If it doesn't have a specific place, then that's why it's clutter and you should go ahead and come up with a place to put it. Drawers, recycling bins, closets, and file cabinets are good places to put stuff. But don't just throw it in the closet and close the door. Organize closets with shelves and cabinets and make sure that drawers are set aside for specific things and file cabinets are carefully labeled.

3 ✿ Freedom-from-oppressive-clutter rule Number 3 is always put things away after you use them. Instead of draping shirts over a chair in your bedroom, hang them up. Dirty clothes can go in a hamper instead of on the floor. Books go back on bookshelves.

4 ✿ Don't wait to put things away until the end of the month. Instead, try to get into a routine for cleaning and picking up around the house (remember from Chapter 4 how enlightening doing mundane things can be?). At the end of each day, pick up, throw away, and organize the small stuff like children's toys, junk mail, daily newspapers, used glasses and mugs and clothes.

5 ✿ Also, don't neglect the yard, which can accumulate its own yard clutter such as trash blown into the shrubs, weeds in the flower bed and too many fallen leaves. Get out and do some pruning.

Word to the Wise

The key to keeping clutter at bay is a combination of picking things up as you go and not having so much junk to begin with.

Storage Options

If your chi isn't cha-cha-ing like it used to, then clearing the clutter may help boost it back up . . . unless you don't have anywhere to put your stuff. That's where storage comes in. The more space you have, the better balanced your chi will be!

We all know drawers, shelves, and cabinets are good places to put stuff, so if you don't have any, get some. If you do have some, maybe it's time to open them up and remove some of the crap in them. Again I repeat, there is no compelling reason to keep every birthday card, coupon, or jar that's ever come through the front door. Being able to part with the past (and all its dust-gathering knick-knacks) is a sign of strength and self-confidence. It means we've shed some light on our souls and we're ready to move on with our lives.

Storage Ideas

1 ✿ The cool kitchen storage available these days is enough to make you learn how to cook something other than brown rice. Head to IKEA, the European chain store that's made an art out of the wicker storage bin, and go for the pullout pantry shelf, brushed aluminum spice rack, stainless steel hooks for hanging pots and pans, and corner-fitting lazy Susans.

2 ✿ Attach trash cans and recycling containers to the inside of cabinet doors or mount them onto pullout racks.

3 ✿ Sew together a series of shoe pouches to fit behind your bedroom door.

4 ✿ Instead of stuffing things under the bed, organize your under bed world with some nice and sturdy wooden boxes. Be sure to attach some small wheels to them to make pulling them out easier.

5 ✿ Large round poster tubes cut down and stacked between two long pieces of wood make for good sock holders.

How to Build Simple Shelves

A good set of shelves can help on your quest to balance your inner energy by overhauling your space. Let's face it: They hold a lot of stuff and once you get rid of your stuff, they make good shrines (see Chapter 1 for details). Making your own simple shelves is also easy to do. It is yet another chance to use your hands and your mind to make something of value and give your soul a solid sense of achievement. How enlightening! The following set of shelves will be roughly six feet high by three feet wide.

You Will Need:

2 6-foot 1 x 10 boards
6 3-foot 1 x 10 boards
4 5-foot metal tracks with clip-in supports
1 sheet of ¼-inch plywood cut 3'1½" x 6'
2-inch finish wood screws
½-inch wood screws (to attach the tracks)

Electric drill
Power saw
Tape measure
Framing square

Steps to Enlightenment

1 ↻ Lay out the two 1 x 10s on the ground and decide which end will be the bottom of the bookcase. Starting at what will be the bottom, measure up 2 inches on both sides of the board and mark each spot with a pencil. Use the framing square as a guide and draw a line across each side of the 1 x 10.

1 ↻ Measure down from the top of each 1 x 10 6 inches on both sides of each board and draw lines at those marks as before.

2 ↻ Stand one 1 x 10 on its side and hold the bottom shelf (a 3-foot 1 x 10) to the inside of the board so that the line falls on the center of the shelf. Attach the shelf by screwing through the face of the 6-foot 1 x 10 and into the end of the shelf. Repeat this process on the other side. Then repeat the process for the top shelf.

3 ↻ You should now have a rectangular box lying face-down on the floor. Make sure the corners are square by measuring diagonally from corner to corner. The two diagonal measurements should be the same. If they're not, it's easy to adjust the box by pushing the top or bottom until the corners are square.

4 ↻ Once all corners are square, lay the plywood on top of the box and secure it by screwing through its face and into the edges of the box along its sides and the top and bottom shelves.

5 ↻ Once the plywood is secure, stand the shelves up. Attach the metal tracks to the insides of the shelves, two on each side spaced about seven inches apart. Clip in the metal supports and fit in the rest of the shelves. Use the power saw to trim shelves as needed to fit into the book shelf.

Going Off the Grid

Pulling the plug at your house in the city and moving the whole kit to Alaska where you can homestead a few acres among the redwoods and the wildlife of God's country has its enlightening moments, but only if you've had success discovering the soulful power of hard work, solar energy, and shitting in the woods. If so, then carving out a home in the wilderness away from the daily grind and constant clatter of city life (as well as the electricity grid) may be just the thing to catch your spirit on fire. Just be careful not to catch your hair on fire. Those who live off the grid tend to have more hair than most of us and in more places.

By the way, you might think that having a long beard (if you're a man) and hairy armpits (if you're a woman) is merely the result of not being able to bathe frequently enough. After all, most water on off-grid homesteads comes from collecting rain and there are gardens to water and animals to feed. Plus rainwater is cold (remember, no hot water heaters).

But the fact is, overgrown hair is one of the side affects of off-grid enlightenment because it means that you're comfortable enough with who you are to not care what others think about you. And anyway, who are you planning to get all spruced up for when you're a hundred miles from the nearest movie theater? If your body odor is making the morning glories wilt, what's the big deal?

Another common question people have when they're thinking of going off-grid is: "Will I start to stockpile weapons to defend myself against the government when they come for me?" The answer to that is no. However, if you choose to homestead alone, with no one to talk to (or reason with) for months and then years, through long cold winters, then the answer to that could become yes. At that point, you may want to consider the fact that the enlightenment you had once felt as you herded your chickens into their pen has run its course. It might be time to head back to the city.

Growing Your Own Food

When you're an hour from the nearest convenience store, growing food at home is going to be important, more so if you're in a cold climate where you have to store food for the winter. Fruit trees (if you're farther south) and berry vines might be good to have around, but they take a long time to get established. Your best bet is to go with a vegetable garden, where you can plant herbs and any number of tasty items like tomatoes, cucumbers, lettuces, carrots, potatoes, and melons. However, the basic vegetable garden consists of what the Native Americans called the Three Sisters: corn, beans, and squash. These crops all work for each other: corn takes nitrogen out of the soil, pole beans put it back in, and squash covers the ground to prevent weeds from growing. When all three are planted together, they imitate the Native American idea of the circle of life, in which all things in nature (including humans) are connected together to help each other survive.

You Will Need:

A plot of land that gets at least five hours of direct sun a day
Compost
Corn kernels
Pole bean and yellow squash seeds
Spade
Water

Steps to Enlightenment

1 ☯ Mound up the dirt in your garden into hills 12 inches high by about 20 inches wide. The mounds should be about 4 feet apart and have flat tops.

2 ☯ Plant five corn kernels in a circle on top of each mound by pushing them into the ground about an inch down. Water the seeds daily.

3 ☯ When the corn seedlings are about 6 inches high (this should take roughly two weeks), plant eight bean seeds on top of each mound in a circle around the corn. Make sure the seeds are about 6 inches away from the corn and equidistant from each other.

4 ☯ One week later, plant eight squash seeds on the sides but near the base of each mound. They should be evenly spaced from one another as well.

5 ☯ Water as necessary and add fertilizer or plant food once a week.

6 ☯ When the corn, beans, and squash begin to grow, pull out the weaker plants so that the strongest grow nice and tall. Then train the pole beans around the corn stalks to give them support.

Word to the Wise

Regardless of where you live, not having electricity means you're going to have to keep food cold in a cold storage shed, which is really just a covered hole in the ground (the ground stays at a cool 50 degrees only several feet down). Some even build cold storage over cold water springs, which does a great job of keeping food cool.

Alternative Power

Getting off the electricity grid doesn't mean you have to go without lights and air-conditioning—at least not all the time. You can hook yourself up to a fully self-contained system of homegrown electricity producers such as solar panels, wind power, and geothermal heating and cooling. Getting started is always the hardest and most expensive part, but think of it as a one-time investment, after which you won't have to pay an electricity bill ever again. Talk about "en-light-ening!"

A List of Alternative Power Sources

1 ✪ Solar power. Harnessing the sun through solar panels (also known as photovoltaic panels) has been around for decades, though it hasn't really caught on as much as it should, mostly because the equipment you need is really expensive. Plus, in order to get a whole house worth of electricity, you'd need a field full of solar panels, which are clunky and not particularly attractive. In the last ten years, individuals and industries have been supplementing their regular power (from the electric grid) with solar panels and this seems to be the way to go. It saves you a little money and you get the uplifting feeling of using nature to power the pump in your backyard goldfish pond.

2 ✪ Wind power. Using windmills to do work has ancient origins. Windmills were used to pump water and grind wheat and other grains into grist for breads. Only in the last 150 years or so have scientists figured out that wind can turn a generator fast enough to produce electricity. The newest models are propeller-like high-speed turbines that have no resemblance whatsoever to the sleepy Dutch model of Don Quixote fame. A common image is a field full of these monsters on the top of a windy western mountain. As with solar power, though, you might consider installing one turbine. Along with your photovoltaics and a little normal power, you'll be a lot closer to going off the grid altogether, which is one step closer to total enlightenment.

3 ✿ Geothermal power. Geothermal power is another old idea, but one that is just now making its way into residential homes. The idea is that under the surface of the earth, the temperature remains at a constant 50 degrees. By drilling down into the earth about 150 feet and feeding flexible plumbing pipe into the hole and back up again you'll be able cool down or heat up water to 50 degrees. Then you can use a heat transfer pump to get the temperature up or you can use a coolant system to chill the water even more. This decreases the amount of work your hot water heater and your heating and air-conditioning system has to do, which means you're using less electricity. And again, if you use geothermal with wind power and solar panels, you'll have a great chance of going off the grid full-time.

Raising Animals

No homestead would be complete without a milk cow and a few chickens running around. The thing is, you can't just go down to the pet store to buy them. Plus, if you're going to keep animals, you're going to have to care for them. Here are some basics on getting started with chickens, a farm animal staple. They offer good eating, eggs, and free fertilizer. Just bear in mind that if you want your chicken flock to grow, you'll have to deal with roosters, which tend to crow at ungodly hours and usually during the daily meditation session.

You Will Need:

A fenced-in area
Covered plywood containers for chicks to sleep in
Old newspaper and wood shavings

250-watt soft-light lightbulb
A 1-gallon water container
2-foot commercial chicken feeder
20 baby chicks

Steps to Enlightenment

1 ✪ Mail-ordering chicks is the best way to get started. You'll be surprised at the number of companies that actually do this.

2 ✪ Before the chicks arrive, use chicken wire (did you expect something else?) and fence off the area where you want the chickens to live. Inside the area, put the plywood containers. Line the floor of the containers with newspaper and wood shavings so they'll have a comfy place to lay their tiny heads. Also, set up the chicken feeder and water container. You might want to consider adding vitamins and minerals to the food and water to make sure the chicks grow strong and fast. One additive made especially for chickens is called—I'm not kidding here—Quick Chick.

3 ✪ When the chicks get there, show them around their new home (especially the water and food areas). Dip their tiny beaks in the water to make sure they know what to do. Keep an eye on the young ones at first and if you notice any really small chicks that don't seem to be growing like the others, it might be necessary to help feed and water them with an eye dropper. Just remember: They're little things, so just give them a drop at a time.

4 ✪ Also, chicks need to be kept warm, so clip a 250-watt lightbulb to the side of their containers and turn it on. Just make sure it's high enough above your feathered friends to avoid having fried friends.

Word to the Wise

To raise the chicks to egg-laying maturity (at which time you'll truly come into an enlightening moment), go out and buy a book on the subject. Then start thinking about that milk cow.

Making Your Own Candles

According to some dream analysts, candles represent protection, spirituality, and guidance. Others say that the color of the candle is important and that, like the colors of feng shui, they can improve your chi or energy in various areas of your life when they're lit. For some, lighting a candle is a way to remember past events and people. In general, candles can shed a warm light in otherwise cold rooms and set a soulful, relaxing mood when the sun goes down and the Tantric sex books come out (whoa Nellie!—see Chapter 7 for more on sexual enlightenment). Adding some essential oils and candles can help fill your house with a fragrant smell, offering sensory stimulation that can heighten your awareness and breed total enlightenment.

You Will Need:

Paraffin wax or beeswax
A double boiler
Wicks
A small metal bolt nut
Popsicle sticks
Two cans taller than you want your candles to be
Wax paper

Steps to Enlightenment

1 ✿ Put the wax in a double boiler and melt it down to liquid form.

2 ✿ While the wax is melting, tie one end of the wick onto the bolt nut and the other end to the middle of a Popsicle stick (which you can hold on to while you lower the wick and nut into the melted wax).

3 ✿ Fill one can with cold water and one can with liquid wax.

4 ✿ Dip the wick with the nut into the wax and pull it out. Then dip it into the water and pull it out. Repeat this process until the candle is at a width you're happy with. If you need to take a break, lay the candle on a sheet of wax paper.

5 ✿ When the dipping is done, lay the candle on a sheet of wax paper to cool for about five hours. During this time, cut off the bottom of the candle to make it flat and to remove the nut.

Word to the Wise

When you take the wax off the double boiler it's going to start to harden. To periodically reliquify the wax, put the can filled with wax into a pot filled with boiling water.

Incense

For thousands of years, incense has been used in both religious ceremonies and medical healing practices in Catholic, Buddhist, Hindu, and shamanic cultures all over the world.

Mostly, incense today comes in cones (which were invented by the Japanese for the Chicago World's Fair in 1898) and joss sticks (named after the Chinese practice of burning incense before a religious idol, or joss). But well before these were invented, incense was anything that burned and had a good smell. Piles of fragrant wood or herbs, herbal pastes and oils were all burned over rocks alongside sacred fires.

Medically speaking, breathing in the smoke from certain burning herbs is believed to have healing powers, especially for Indian Ayurvedic practices (class-action tobacco lawsuits notwithstanding). Incense burning during religious ceremonies also takes on special meaning, especially for Hindus. They believe that since incense is made from nature (wood, herbs, flowers) and that God and nature are one, burning incense is a way to personally connect with the gods. That's why when you walk the streets of Katmandu, Nepal, a city with a majority of Hindus, the smoky smell of *nag* or incense is a constant. It is lit morning and evening as part of the daily *puja* and there is always a stick burning in the local temple.

Burning incense in the house is another way to align your chi, as mapped out with a feng shui *bagua,* because of how certain incense ingredients align with the elements (according to Ayurvedic practices). Sandalwood, aloeswood, cedarwood, cassia, frankincense, and myrrh fall under the water element. Tumeric, ginger, valerian, and Indian spikenard are earth scents. Clove holds fire energy while patchouli symbolizes air. Even if you don't feel like aligning your chi, incense can help improve a calming atmosphere inside your living space while lending an air of mystical enlightenment—perfect for the weekly Wicca meeting.

How to Make Your Own Incense

You Will Need:

2 parts Makko, a natural binding agent made from the bark of
   the tabu-no-ki tree in Asia
1 part sandalwood powder
1 part cassia powder
½ part clove powder

A cup or two of warm water
A medium-sized mixing bowl
A 2-foot-by-2-foot flat surface covered in wax paper
6-inch narrow bamboo sticks

Steps to Enlightenment

1 ☯ Put all dry ingredients in mixing bowl and mix them thoroughly together.

2 ☯ Add little bits of water and knead mixture into a moist gummy dough.

3 ☯ Roll up a ping-pong–sized ball of dough and poke a bamboo stick about a ½ inch into the ball of dough. Put the dough and stick down on the wax paper and roll it into a long thin stick of incense, taking care not to let it come off the bamboo stick.

4 ☯ Allow the incense to dry for 72 hours before burning.

Word to the Wise

If you can't buy powdered ingredients, get a mortar and pestle and grind them out yourself. This may even be the preferred way to go since you'll be assured that the ingredients will be fresh. Plus, this way you can put on your witch's hat and start mixing in sage, rosemary, and bergamot oil, which is a magic potion for turning your man or woman into a love machine. Then you'll really gain some enlightening chi.

Zen Rock Gardening

The Japanese form of gardening has always evoked a sense of calm meditation because of the way it is anchored by big, heavy, soulful rocks. That said, you can't just throw a few rocks down on the ground and be done with it. Japanese landscapers take great care with the type of rocks they use, their shape and size and their placement. The idea is to create the look of a mountain setting or streambed, with the one rule being that it must look natural, not linear or formal like the rigid lines found in English gardens.

One type of Japanese gardening style that was influenced by Zen Buddhist monks is called Karensansui or "dry mountain stream" gardens. In these popular landscapes, white gravel or sand is poured around large rocks to mimic flowing water lapping at the shores of mountainous islands. By raking the sand around the rocks in smooth simple curves, garden maintenance becomes daily meditation.

You Will Need:

Several large rocks of the same color and consistency (it's also impor-
    tant that these rocks are completely natural and not hand cut)
White sand, or if that's not available, crushed granite or pea gravel
A few able bodies

Steps to Enlightenment

1 ✿ Take note of the flow and space of your garden and how it relates to any nearby structures. You don't want any rocks to go higher than the roofline of the house (bad feng shui) and you don't want to place rocks where they're going to be intrusive or in the way (more bad feng shui).

2 ✿ Put down a weed barrier over the entire space you plan to cover with stones and sand. There's nothing serene about weeds poking up through what is supposed to be calm flowing water.

3 ✿ Place the rocks. The idea is to make groupings of rocks. Place the tallest and largest rock at the center of each group and surround it with smaller rocks. The classic Zen gardens have groupings of three or four rocks symbolizing the Buddha stone, the goddess stone, and the child stone. Stone shapes and their names include the soul stone, a vertical stone with a wide base and a tapered top; the body stone, another vertical stone whose base is only slightly wider than its top; and the heart stone, a flat and wide rock. The body stone is always the tallest in the garden and together these shapes offer interesting contrasts to one another.

4 ✿ Pour and shovel the sand, crushed granite, or pea gravel into place. This should be about two inches thick around the garden.

5 ✿ Rake the sand. There are various patterns you can use to create visually appealing lines in a rock garden. Usually, the sand is raked in lines parallel to the house and close around each rock as if they were touching the water and sending out concentric rings. While you're raking, be sure to plan for how you will exit the garden without having to leave footprints in your newly raked sand.

Word to the Wise

Moss is an important part of Zen rock gardens and you should encourage it to grow on your rocks over the years. You can encourage moss to grow by spreading a bit of wet potter's clay on the rocks before transplanting some moss from your local gardening store. Be sure and mist the moss daily to keep it going.

Installing a Backyard Water Element

There is some argument as to whether the sound of trickling water over Zen-gray river stones is meditative or just reason for having to get up three times a night to take a piss. Regardless, the use of water in Japanese gardening has always had spiritual meaning. Even before the advent of potting plants and building carefully winding pathways in Japanese backyards, rocks and water were used to section off sacred ground and symbolize the presence of nature's spirits. Modern Japanese gardening still uses these two elements to create calming settings where a person can get back to nature, even if he or she happens to live in the big, soulless city.

You Will Need:

Spade shovel
Pickax
Length of nylon rope
Sand
Rubberized liner
Utility knife
Length of 2 x 4 lumber
3-foot level
Submersible pump
Electrical outlet/source of electricity

Steps to Enlightenment

1 ✿ Use a length of nylon rope and lay it out on the ground in the location and shape of the pond. Many aquatic plants, including the sacred lotus flower, need lots of direct sunlight, so you'll want to locate the

pond where it will get good sun during the day. Also, putting a pond next to trees is a nice idea, but there will be roots to dig around and that's a much more difficult job. And finally, don't put a pond right next to your house's foundation where water can seep out and cause a world of trouble—we're going for tranquility here, not catastrophe.

2 ✿ Mark the shape of the pond in the ground by scraping away the top soil with your shovel just inside the nylon rope outline.

3 ✿ Use a shovel, pickax, or other digging tools to dig out a hole for the pond. You'll want to put shallow shelves around the perimeter of the pond to grow shallow-water plants and a deeper middle to grow other types of plants like lotus flowers. The shelves should be a foot below the surface and at least a foot wide. The rest of the pond should be between two and three feet deep. Be sure and slope the sides.

4 ✿ Once you have your hole dug, check to make sure the ground around the pond is level. Do this by placing a length of 2 x 4 over the pond and placing a 3-foot level on top of that. If one side is lower than another, you'll have water pouring over that edge, which will not help to calm your soul. Use the excavated soil from the hole you just dug to build up low sides.

5 ✿ Next, smooth out the bottom and sides of the pond, removing any sharp stones or jagged roots.

6 ✿ Spread two inches of sand along the bottom, sides, and shelves of the pond.

7 ✿ Lay a rubberized liner over the pond and fit it as best you can to the contours of the hole. Allow at least 12 inches of the liner to come up and over the pond's sides. Weigh the liner down with rocks.

8 ✿ If you want a natural looking bottom, now's the time to cover the liner with stone, sand, or whatever you like.

9 ✿ Cover the edges of the liner with dirt or flat stone, which makes for a nice finishing touch as well. Trim excess liner with a utility knife.

10 ✿ To build a waterfall next to the pond, place a submersible pump at the lowest part of the pond and run a length of flexible PVC pipe to the spot where you want the waterfall. Hide the pipe (along with the pump's electrical cord) under soil or behind rocks.

11 ✿ Stack rocks around the pump hose so that it will empty at the top of the stack. The best way to direct water down the rocks and back into the pond is to stack larger rocks at the bottom and smaller ones at the top. Using a large flat rock is a good way to get a natural cascade back into the pool of water.

12 ✿ Fill the pond with a garden hose to about 4 inches below the top. To activate the waterfall, turn on the pump and adjust the rocks around the pump hose to get the look (and sound) you're after.

Word to the Wise

After you dig the hole for the pond, use the dirt to create landscaping berms or flower beds around the body of water.

This is all that I've known for certain, that God is love. Even if I
have been mistaken on this or that point: God is nevertheless love.

—Søren Kierkegaard

SEVEN

Soul Mating

The thing about love is that it is almost universally recognized as being a powerful, life-changing force, and because of that many people in the world point to love as the one true religion. In fact, most religions, if not all of them, talk about love in the same sentence as they talk about God. For some, like Kierkegaard, God and Love are interchangeable. If I have love then I have God, one might say. That's why love and partnership is as least as sought after as a spiritual life, because when we're in love our souls are as full as they'll ever be.

How to Find Your Soul Mate

Finding a soul mate is kind of a misleading prospect, because it implies finding someone who is perfect (i.e., no difference in opinion, good looks, nice family, doesn't snore, etc.). But that's not the case. Usually a soul mate is someone who has come into your life to give you a gift, whether that gift is helping you to realize love, to achieve a goal, or to teach you some important lesson so you can improve your karma and

up your next life's allotment. In other words, there's plenty of room for imperfection and even outright combat. Nevertheless, the search for someone special—as is the case with all journeys of the soul—can lead to enlightening ends.

Of course, there's more to finding a soul mate than making sure you don't have spinach in your teeth after a dinner date. It takes work. But not work in the sense of trying out new singles bars or signing up for ten different online dating services. The focus here is work on the self. For example, if you're still dealing with past emotional wounds or sexual hang-ups, find yourself a good therapist, preferably one with an Eastern European accent that can channel Freud. If you're short on the $150 an hour it takes to see an Eastern European therapist, try twelve-step programs like Al-Anon, where piecing together lives and dealing with the past is business as usual. In short, do what it takes to learn enough about yourself, find confidence in your emotions, and get yourself centered. Only then will you be ready for love, both how to give it and how to receive it. No love, no soul mate, simple as that.

The only drawback to centering yourself and finding peace with who you are, is that everyone—soul mate or not—is going to be eager to get to know you, some more intimately than others (which is always an enlightening prospect in its own right, but let's not lose focus here). However, what you're looking for in a soul mate is someone who's been working on themselves in the same way you have been. Otherwise, you'll be dealing with the emotional past all over again, only it won't be yours.

How to Tell If Someone Has Worked on Themselves

1 ☯ They have the perfect abs.

2 ☯ They speak in calm clear sentences instead of rambling treatises (unless much red wine has been drunk, in which case rambling treatises can be romantic).

3 ☯ They look you in the eyes when they talk to you.

4 ☯ They're not too eager to jump in the sack. If they are, they may not be your soul mate, but in some cases so what? There's nothing wrong with a little slap and tickle on your way to a perfectly harmonious relationship.

5 ☯ They don't flinch at the implication of long-term commitment. To check this, casually say the words "marriage" and "children" in conversation, preferably when your date is taking a drink of water, and note what happens. Spewing water or gagging and coughing is a bad sign. A subtle yet noticeable widening of the eyes followed by stuttered talk is some cause for alarm, but worthy of further investigation. If he or she takes the conversation in stride with no visible shudder, the signs are good.

Word to the Wise

Many times finding a soul mate is more like running into an old friend; you just know it when it happens in a sort of love-at-first-sight type way. Because of that, you might have better luck locating that special someone if you just stop looking for him or her altogether and continue to focus on becoming who you are.

The Perfect Date

There's something to be said for the old-fashioned way of arranged marriages, where your family decided who you were going to spend the rest of your life with. You didn't have to wait for a secret message to arrive at your door from that someone special (the equivalent these days is waiting by the phone). There was no restless hoping that he or she thinks you're smart and good looking (for those who were neither smart nor good looking this was the best deal they could imagine). In fact, you didn't have to worry whether he or she would like you at all—you just showed up at the wedding day, tied the knot and started what must have been a very awkward and exciting period of getting to know each other.

All that said, there was one major drawback to arranged marriages: The large chance of not actually being in love with the person you were going to marry. These days, not loving the person you plan to marry is usually considered a very large red-flag warning sign. And that's why we date. Unfortunately some dates go great and some go dismally.

How to Know You're on the Perfect Date

1 ✿ The date is out of the ordinary. If you're in a hot air balloon sipping champagne and nibbling strawberries, rest assured that the date is going to be interesting at the very least, if not downright perfect. This means whoever set up the date is imaginative, romantic, and fun. It also means he or she is trying to impress you, which is nice. Dinner and a movie, on the other hand, should be reserved for married couples with kids who long for such peace and normalcy.

2 ✿ You can't say the wrong thing to the right person. On a great date, you'll never feel annoyed or feel as though you're annoying. And if you

do happen to stick your foot in your mouth and it invokes a laugh from your partner, then you're on the perfect date.

3 ✿ Silence is as comfortable as conversation. If there's a lull in the conversation during a beautiful sunset as a pair of swans glides in for a landing and you don't feel uncomfortable or nervous, you can put another check in the "yes" column.

4 ✿ You gain some enlightenment while on the date. Even if you won't be spending the rest of your life with this person and he or she manages to open your eyes to something new and magical in the world, it's a good date.

Word to the Wise

There comes a time in life when you become ready to meet the right person for all the right reasons. Being ready does not include needing someone to help make you whole (that will have come before Mr. or Mrs. Right steps into the picture). Also, being ready to meet the right person does not include needing someone to save you, support you, or help you stabilize your emotional life or your standing among family and friends. All that is part of your personal path to enlightenment. The right person will help you continue on your path of personal fulfillment and that's what you can look out for when you start dating.

The Not-So-Perfect Date

Not everyone you meet is going to be soul mate material and if you find yourself wishing they are on every date you go on, then perhaps a little more time with your own soul is in order. Most of the time you'll go out on dates with some great people—just not soul mates. And then sometimes, you'll go out with really awful people and a half hour into the date you'll find yourself preferring to drink an old coffee can full of wood screws instead of carrying on with the laborious, soul-draining night.

How to Know You're on the Not-So-Perfect Date

1 ✪ Your date shows up with spinach in his or her teeth and you spend the first hour of the date trying to figure out ways you can point out the fact to him or her in a way that won't be too embarrassing for either of you.

2 ✪ Halfway through the date, you get into an argument.

3 ✪ He or she says things like, "We'll have to change the way you do that."

4 ✪ You share various enlightening moments with your date and he or she laughs cynically and says, "Yeah right, and I'm the pope."

5 ✪ Your hair catches on fire.

6 ✪ You accidentally spill some laxatives in your date's mai tai and forget to tell him or her.

7 ✪ You find yourself unexpectedly needing to rush to the bathroom at your date's house to empty your bowels and you discover that the toilet is filthy and there is no toilet paper.

Word to the Wise

A big trap many people fall into when a date isn't going well is trying to figure out how the other person feels, but this is impossible. The fact is, we can only know how we feel when we're around someone else. If we start to feel angry, depressed, sad, or vulnerable during a date, then there's a good chance that there are issues inside us that are keeping us from personal freedom. For that reason, dating can be about self-realization, as long as we pay attention to and learn from our own emotions as we interact with other people. Blaming ourselves for how someone else feels or worrying how others feel will only lead to not-so-perfect dates.

Enlightenment Through Sex

Does this really need an explanation? Well, yes, because lots of people have sex, but most don't have spiritualized sex. That's why long ago, the Hindus adopted Tantric sex and the Kama Sutra as part of their religion. By doing that, they made sex not only okay to have but required to have if you want to reach enlightenment. Now we're talking! Plus, the sex that's advocated in Tantric literature and in the Kama Sutra isn't of the pious missionary kind, no sir. They pulled out all the stops and created some of the nuttiest positions this side of Bangkok . . . all in the name of transcendence! Well done.

Tantric Sex

Like yoga dining, Tantric sex is about slowing down and tasting every juicy minute of sex with your partner in order to tap into that essential life energy that exists in all of us. In this case, that energy is sexual.

With a history that dates back to ancient Egypt, Tantric sex seeks to harness sexual energy by controlling it. Rather than wham-bam-thank-you-ma'am, get it over with and I'm outta here sex, partners are encouraged to treat the physical act of sex as a sacred event where every touch, action, and perception is done in complete ritual awareness. With this kind of intense concentration, partners can lengthen each sexual session and savor the growing sensual energy and enlightenment that accompanies intense orgasms.

You Will Need:

A partner (optional)
Some healthy, juicy fruit
Privacy
Candles
Massage oils
Feathers or silk scarves

Steps to Enlightenment

1 ✺ Even with Tantric sex there's no getting around foreplay. In fact, most of Tantric sex is foreplay. Light some candles and perhaps a little incense. Then have a bath and gently bathe each other. As you consciously caress each (and every!) body part, think of your partner as a god or goddess. Empty your mind of worry and anything else that gets in the way of complete awareness of your partner's physical body.

2 ✺ Without getting dressed, try eating some juicy fruits, honey, or fish (all of which are known as—wait for it—"genital" foods). Needless to say, it's okay for the fruit juice and honey to get on you. Oh Nellie!

3 ✺ Then get out the oil and gently spread it on each other. Spiritually speaking, this can be considered the anointing (not annoying) stage. Physically, this can be considered the really fantastic stage.

4 ✺ During or after the oil part (which, by the way, can go on for as long as is deemed necessary), try caressing each other with the feathers and silk scarves.

Important: By this point, you may feel the urge to ditch the feathers and the oil and get down to some serious sex, but stop yourself. Revel in the sexual energy you're feeling and hold on to it. This is what Tantric sex is all about.

5 ✿ After the lengthy foreplay, now's the time for, ahem, intercourse (assuming the male partner is, ahem, erect). The man should put his penis just inside his partner's vagina and without pushing in farther, just leave it there for a whole minute.

6 ✿ After a minute, the man should pull his penis out and rest it on the woman's clitoral area for another minute or longer, after which he should go back inside his partner.

7 ✿ This process is repeated over and over and each time the couple should lie still while caressing each other and being fully aware of their physical union. If the urge to have an orgasm approaches either partner (and it most definitely will), then they should recognize this urge but pull back from it. The idea is to come close to orgasm but not go over the edge in order to achieve an ongoing intense level of sexual pleasure.

Word to the Wise

The key to staving off orgasm during a Tantric sex session is steady breathing and staying focused, not unlike what you would do during a yoga session.

The Kama Sutra

This ancient Hindu love manual was written by a man named Vatsya-yana in the third or fourth century CE and many of the steamy positions and sexual suggestions inside it came from an earlier book known as the *Kama Shastras* or *Rules of Love*. The original purpose of the book was not as the first form of smut, but rather as a guide to fulfilling the message of Kama, the Hindu God of Love. Kama is a little like Cupid, except a little more racy. He's the son of the goddess Lakshmi and shoots a five-headed, flower-tipped arrow at people to arouse their five senses and enlighten the mind with visions of beauty (and in the case of the Kama Sutra, visions of various kinky sexual positions).

The book is divided into seven sections that include suggestions for coming on to a woman, how to find a bride, and then how to get it on with other men's wives (!). There are also suggestions for aphrodisiacs and of course an illustrated section on various Tantras or positions (there is no relation here to Tantric sex practices). While there are hundreds of positions detailed, some of which only the most acrobatic among us could ever even hope to accomplish, including one involving ropes, pulleys, and a harness, our man Vatsyayana is pious enough to point out that a truly spiritual sexual experience should involve no more than three during any one session. And you thought this was the easy way to achieve enlightenment . . .

Enlightening Sexual Positions from the Kama Sutra

1 ✪ Aphrodite's Delight. "Catch hold of her two feet, raising them till they press upon her breasts and her legs form a rough circle."

2 ✪ The Lotus. "Sit facing your lover and grasp her ankles, fastening them like a chain behind your neck. She then grips her toes as you make love."

3 ✪ The Knot of Flame. "Sitting erect, grip your lover's waist and pull her on to you, your loins continuously leaping together with a sound like the flapping of elephants' ears."

4 ✪ Suspended. "The woman sits in her lover's cradled hands, her arms around his neck, thighs gripping his waist and her feet pushing back and forth against a wall."

5 ✪ Two Palms. "The man leans back to a wall and his lover clings to his neck while placing both her feet in his palms while making love."

6 ✪ **The Knee Elbow.** "You lift your lover by passing your elbows under her knees and gripping her buttocks while she hangs fearfully from your neck."

How to Love Unconditionally

The true indication that you've found your soul mate is not the willingness to perform a few of the positions in the Kama Sutra (though soul mates are not necessarily required for such spiritual explorations), but rather in the ease with which he or she can love you, warts and all, through lean years and fat years and with total trust even as your ego tries to butt its way in. This is what it means to love unconditionally. It is perhaps the hardest thing to attain in a relationship and those that do achieve unconditional love have reached the milestone after much personal enlightenment on their own.

Sometimes giving love unconditionally is easy and there is an ease and a joy in being around the person you love every day. Sometimes, however, there are people that you do truly love, but for one reason or another it has become hard to connect with or difficult to always show them how you feel (I'm thinking family members here). In that case, you can transcend those difficulties by doing the following letterwriting exercise.

You Will Need:

A pen
Some paper
An open heart

Steps to Enlightenment

1 ✪ When you sit down to write, just remember not to qualify the love you're feeling. Saying things like, "I would love you so much more if you hadn't sold my comic book collection" doesn't help. Also, don't bring up what it is you're angry about and don't lapse into blame. Simply go to the place in your heart where there is only love for the person you're thinking about and tell them about that love. This is about giving freely of yourself.

2 ✪ Write about a past joyful time with the person. Tell them that you remember the joy and closeness you felt then and tell them that you still carry that feeling with you.

3 ✪ Describe the things about them that you love. "I love the way you laugh through your nose" or "My heart fills up when you tuck your napkin into your shirt at expensive restaurants."

4 ✪ After you get the letter written, put it in a plain envelope and put it in the mail. Dropping it off will only risk confrontation. Adding in rose petals, glitter, or a sticker that says "I 'heart' you" will only distract attention from the words in the letter.

Word to the Wise

Before you even sit down to write this letter, get it in your head not to expect anything in return. This exercise is about you living the idea of unconditional love. Whether they respond or not doesn't matter. What does matter is that you've given your love to them.

Enlightenment Through Marriage

Getting married is actually something of a relief. You no longer have to worry about finding a soul mate (hopefully). You can retire from the dating singles game (hopefully). And you now have a good excuse to pass up that fifth tequila shot (hopefully). In other words, when you get married, you start a whole new chapter.

Also, getting married gives you access to a special but never talked about married club. Your parents and their friends will start treating you like a responsible adult. You'll get a raise at work. Banks and mortgage companies will start trying to become your best friend. And all the while, no one will ever consciously recognize this subtle change. You will just be silently initiated into greater responsibility and debt.

But that's not why marriage is enlightening. With marriage comes a new kind of relationship with your partner. After a commitment like this, you'll both grow closer. Trust will begin to blossom into a permanent bloom. As the years go by, you will add memories and experiences together while always having someone with whom you can share your own newfound nuggets of truth. By getting married you choose a life companion and instead of having one set of eyes and one heart to search with, you'll have two. It's as if your souls have intertwined and you become one.

Marriage Ceremonies

The wedding ceremony is a celebration of two people's union. This is the time to share your enlightenment with others and to stand up in front of God and everyone (even if everyone is the Justice of the Peace and his wife), proclaim your commitment to each other and announce your new way of life.

Weddings are often tied to religions and faith as they are considered sacred in many areas of the world. In fact, Hindu men believe that they won't be able to achieve the highest goals of their religion (i.e., total enlightenment) unless they get married. Some, like the Buddhists, simply want to merge their spiritual paths with their personal lives (is there a difference?).

We're all familiar with Christian weddings that take place in a church with a priest, though you'd be forgiven if you couldn't find similarities in all of them. Some invoke Jesus in a Catholic cathedral while others invoke Native American spirits under an oak tree with a certified massage therapist guiding the ceremony. The ceremonies we aren't so familiar with are those belonging to the world's other major religions. Compared to most Christian ceremonies these can really blow the lid off your soul.

Hinduism

Hindu weddings are very important, sacramental events for both men and women. It is thought that Hindu men need to get hitched in order to grow their faiths (and their lives). Women gain from marriage too, least of all because they're suppose to get money and jewelry from the groom's family before the special day.

These weddings are colorful, raucous affairs that can last weeks on end, with party after party, street processions, outrageous dress, and some body painting. If you're lucky enough to get invited to one, be sure and go. The party alone is going to make your soul dance, never mind the wonderfully elaborate wedding ceremony. If this is the wedding you're going to have, check with the person who plans to bankroll the party and make sure they can get a loan.

You Will Need:

Copies of the bride and groom's horoscopes
A horse (preferably white)
A Hindu priest (preferably jaunty)
A band that can walk and play at the same time
A fire
Uncooked raw rice (three handfuls)
Two garlands of flowers (one for the bride and one for the groom)
One statue of Ganesh, the Elephant God
Traditional Hindu dress (a kurta for the man; a sari for the woman)
1 tablespoon red powder, or *sindoor*
1 tablespoon turmeric
Some blessed water in a fancy cup

Steps to Enlightenment

1 ✿ Before the wedding, tradition has it that the bride and groom's horoscopes are read and documented by a licensed astrologer. The astrologer is then asked to compare the two to make sure they are compatible. If not, the whole thing is called off. In light of potential incompatibilities, it is recommended to get the horoscopes done well before the temple is booked. Either that or pay the astrologer a little extra—nudge, nudge, wink, wink—to make sure they are compatible.

2 ✿ Assuming the stars line up, the ceremony starts with the groom arriving at the wedding site on a horse after a long procession that has wound through the local streets. Joining the groom is his family, friends, and all the rest of the wedding guests, except the bride and the bride's family, both of whom will meet the procession at the wedding site. A band should join in the procession and everyone should make loads of noise, while dancing and having a generally good old time.

3 ✿ Once at the wedding site, a Hindu priest asks Ganesh to remove any obstacles in the way of the ceremony.

4 ✿ Next, the father of the bride hands her over to the groom in a cere-mony known as the Kanya Daan. He first rubs turmeric on his daugh-ter's hands to symbolize her change in status from single to married and then he puts his daughter's hand in the groom's hand. Afterward, he pours out some holy water to symbolize that he has washed his hands of his daughter (a truly symbolic gesture, seeing as he's about to spend the next five years paying off her elaborate wedding party).

5 ✿ To show his thanks, the groom promises the father that he will help his daughter to achieve dharma or total enlightenment (yes, it's true).

6 ✿ Then the jaunty priest ties the bride and groom's clothes together to show that they are one.

7 ✿ The bride and groom exchange garlands.

8 ✿ The marriage fire is then lit and the bride then throws three hand-fuls of rice into the altar fire as an offering to the flame (the fire repre-sents the divine witness to the wedding). It's common for the bride's brother or another male relative to pour the rice in the bride's hand as a gesture of good will.

9 ✿ The couple then takes the seven steps (known as the *sapta padi*). After each step a blessing or prayer is recited by the bride or groom. These prayers include asking for strength, sustenance, and good luck. After the seven steps the couple is husband and wife.

10 ✿ To show the bride's change in status, the groom puts red powder known as *sindoor* in the part of the bride's hair.

11 ✿ The wedding party then sprinkles flower petals over the newly married couple to bless them and to ward off evil.

Buddhism

For Buddhists of long ago, getting married was not part of the path to nirvana and in fact was considered by some as yet another form of suffering (those in not so great marriages may tend to agree). For that reason, they never created a marriage ceremony. Still, that hasn't stopped modern-day Buddhists from tying the knot using the faith's scriptures and chants to bless the union. It's a simple ceremony, of course, and you'll need to make it legal at the courthouse, if that's what you want. Buddhists believe that if you're serious about wanting a family life and honoring your partner, then there's no need to make the marriage formal.

You Will Need:

An open time slot with a Buddhist monk or lama
A food offering to the monk
A Buddhist temple and/or a shrine to Buddha
Two candles
Incense
Two cups, one larger than the other, filled with sake

Steps to Enlightenment

1 ✷ Before the wedding, show up at your appointed time with the Buddhist monk and ask him to bless your decision to enter into family life. As you do this, present the monk with some food (try to present it on a tray in a nice way; a paper sack of McDonald's is not going to get you a blessing).

2 ✷ After the blessing, head down to the temple unless you're already there. Now the ceremony begins. Monks at the temple chant from scriptures (the most common chants are used to honor Buddha, the Enlightened One). The bride and groom stand before a shrine holding a statue of Buddha.

3 ✷ After the chants, the two candles that have been placed on the shrine are lit by the bride and groom's families to symbolize the union of each family.

4 ✷ Friends and other family members can then approach the shrine and light incense as an offering to the couple.

5 ✷ The couple then drinks from the smaller cup of sake and then the larger cup. This symbolizes the growing union of the couple.

6 ✷ A priest or official steeped in Buddhist teachings then guides the ceremony by leading the bride and groom through the vows. Vows can be made up by the couple and mostly they consist of questions like, "Will you honor your husband/wife?," "Will you remain faithful?," etc. At the end, he pronounces the couple husband and wife.

7 ✷ The priest can then remind the couple and the audience of the impermanence of worldly things, of compassion for all living things, and of the importance of staying on the path to enlightenment.

Islam

Muslim wedding ceremonies are relatively quick affairs. It's the parties surrounding the ceremony that seem to hold the most potential for enlightening fun in the name of loving union. In this light, Islamic customs are similar to Hindu customs. Parties can start weeks before the wedding and the big feast after is the place to see and be seen, assuming you live in a more enlightened Muslim country and not, say, rural Afghanistan or Pakistan, where the women are separated from the men like a junior high school cotillion.

You Will Need:

Henna ink and applicators
A band
Some friends who like to dance
Some drums
An imam
Food enough for a feast

Steps to Enlightenment

1 ✪ A week before the wedding day, the bride and groom's families hold one big party called a *dholki*, during which friends and family gather to play the drums and dance and sing. Food aplenty is spread out and the parties last through the night. Having more than one *dholki* is fine, as long as you don't *dholki* through the wedding ceremony.

2 ✪ Three days before the big day, the bride goes to a henna ceremony in which all the women, including the bride, have their hands and feet painted in impermanent tattoos known as henna tattoos. This ceremony is called the Mehendi and it, too, is loud, festive, and colorful,

with the women dressed in bright but traditional formal shalwarka-meez outfits. After this, tradition says that the bride isn't supposed to leave the house until the wedding day.

3 ✪ Next is the wedding ceremony itself. The groom arrives in the *baraat,* which is a loud procession of guests and family and a band. It's supposed to be a festive event, and often is.

4 ✪ After the *baraat,* the bride and groom exchange vows, agreeing to honor and love each other and pay each other's credit card bills. There is much reading from the Koran by the imam. Traditional costumes are worn, with the bride donning several pounds of gold jewelry as well as a traditional veil, adjusted so that it doesn't hide the gold. The groom can sport a crown of roses, a turban, or a fine tailored suit, whichever toots his horn (or more likely his bride's horn).

5 ✪ After the wedding, a big feast called the *valima* is thrown by the groom's family during which everyone fills their plates, dances, and drinks too much all in the name of loving unions.

Judaism

Compared to Hindu, Muslim, and even Buddhist weddings, Jewish weddings can seem about as exciting as a box of hammers, especially if the bride and groom happen to practice Orthodox Judaism. Instead of feasting, the bride and groom fast on their wedding day. Bright colors are out and white is in. There is no singing, only solemn caution-ary words from the rabbi. In fact, the peak of excitement for the bride may come the day before the wedding when she gets symbolically cleansed of her sins in a bathhouse somewhere near her great aunt's house. Granted, once the wedding ceremony itself is over with, there can be a great party with much Jewish line dancing.

You Will Need:

A ring
A chuppah or four-cornered tent
A rabbi
A bottle of wine and two glasses
A glass wrapped in cloth
A secluded spot to spend some time after the ceremony

Steps to Enlightenment

1 ✪ We've talked a little about the events leading up to a traditional Jewish ceremony. If you can think of more fun ways to do this, then more power to you. A rehearsal dinner might be a good place to start. Orthodox shmorthodox.

2 ✪ Another fun thing to do might be to have a ceremony during which the bride and groom sign the Ketubah, which is a traditional document stating the couples' commitment to each other and to their faith. These documents can be very elaborate, making for good framed art for the living room (and eventually the upstairs hallway).

3 ✪ The big thing during the ceremony is the chuppah, which is a tent or canopy under which the bride and groom get married. It is supposed to symbolize the home the new couple will make together.

4 ✪ After the couple walk separately to the chuppah with their families, the rabbi reads the vows. Then the bride walks around the groom a symbolic seven times. This can represent several different things though many people consider this a way for the bride to create a magical aura around the groom to protect him from evil (and the glances of other women). My question is, what about the bride?! The groom is protected from evil, but she has to wander the streets vulnerable to the catcalls

of construction workers and the barbs of daily newspaper headlines?! Perhaps a little encircling by the groom is in order here.

5 ↻ Once the circling is over, the groom steps on the glass inside the cloth and breaks it to signify that the new couple has passed the point of no return (the broken glass cannot be mended).

6 ↻ Following the ceremony, as the after party begins, the bride and groom usually spend about twenty minutes alone, away from the party. This is called the Yichud and it's a time for the couple to collect themselves, take a deep breath, kiss a little, have a bite to eat, and reflect on why Aunt Edna wore such a loud purple dress.